Breakaway
Wisdom

LIFE STRATEGIES FROM THE COACHES OF HOCKEY EAST

Foreword by Nancy Murrapese-Burrell,
Boston Globe

JOHN LEAHY

PAGE PUBLISHING
Conneaut Lake, PA

First originally published by Page Publishing 2024

ISBN 979-8-89157-100-6 (pbk)
ISBN 979-8-89157-132-7 (digital)

Printed in the United States of America

CONTENTS

ACKNOWLEDGMENTS

Any time a book is written, the author seldom works alone, and that certainly is the case with this book. I am indebted to so many great folks who gave me their time and attention in completing this work. First and foremost, I would like to thank the twelve ice hockey coaches of Hockey East who were so cooperative in giving me a few minutes of their time at the respective campuses around the league. This book could not have been completed without them, and to a large extent it *is* about them.

You will notice that there are two interviews in this book that were conducted with coaches from the University of Massachusetts. At the time the book was launched, the Minutemen were coached by Don "Toot" Cahoon. During the production of this work, Coach Cahoon tendered his resignation with the program and was subsequently replaced by John Micheletto. I have included both interviews here, to fully embrace the ideas of both men and enhance the work. I'd like to thank UMass for their flexibility and cooperation.

Additionally, at the time of this book's original publication, the University of Connecticut had yet to be a member of Hockey East. I have since added a chapter to include the Huskies, represented by their head coach, Mike Cavanaugh, to ensure inclusion of all the men's teams.

Also, at the time of the initial publication, I was broadcasting exclusively covering the men's games for Merrimack. Consequently, all the interviews for this book were conducted with men's coaches. This is no way intended as a slight to the women's game and their coaches, and I am proud to say I am now intensively involved with the women's game, broadcasting both men's and women's hockey for Merrimack on ESPN+.

A big thank you goes out to the sports information contacts and support people around the league, who were absolutely critical to the success of this project by scheduling the coaches to meet with me: Jorge Rocha, Alastair Ingram, Brad Davis, Mark Majewski, Lisa Kennedy, Jillian Jakuba, Laura Reed, Sean Hladick, Brian Kelley, Tom Wilkins, Christina Coleman, Tim Clark, and Colin Stewart. It never ceases to amaze me at the way each one of you handles your crazy workload. I am forever in your debt.

I'd also like to thank Nancy Murrapese-Burrell of the Boston Globe for being willing to share a few thoughts in the foreword section of the book. Nancy is a regular at Hockey East arenas, and it is always great to see her when she comes to Merrimack. It's always great talking to her.

Lastly and mostly, I'd like to give a big shout out to my wife Lori-Ann. She has been such a huge source of support for me, and I am so grateful that she is good enough to understand my busy schedule and is willing to back me as I strive to succeed in this crazy business of sports. I salute you all.

F O R E W O R D

Those of us who cover Hockey East are blessed to work with some of the best and brightest in college hockey. The commitment of the coaches, the determination and sacrifice of the players, and the pride and tradition that define the programs comprise what makes the sport so phenomenal.

It is a privilege to be around the enthusiasm surrounding all eleven Hockey East teams. No one is more energized and excited about his job than John Leahy, who lends his broadcasting expertise as the voice of Merrimack hockey.

Leahy takes a rare look inside the inner workings of the coaches' offices and his passion for writing is as strong as his love of hockey.

Nancy Murrapese-Burrell, Boston Globe

INTRODUCTION

This is a book about success, plain and simple. But unlike the vast majority of success and self-help books out there, this volume will have a very unique twist to it. You are about to experience success by looking through the lens of twelve college hockey coaches. These twelve men are the bench bosses of the teams that comprise Hockey East, one of the most competitive and elite college hockey conferences in the country. I sat down and interviewed these coaches on specific topics of success that I handpicked at each of the eleven venues of the league. These are the concepts that I feel are the most critical to achieving what we know as success. Maybe the elements of success are different to you—a concept that I feel is necessary component may not be applicable for you. That's okay. The point is that each coach was able to give me specific and detailed thoughts about what the particular concept means to him, both in general and as it relates to the team he coaches.

You will learn, for example, how Jerry York, a man who has won multiple national championships, looks at confidence. You will learn Jack Parker's approach to the topic of focus with his Boston University squad. You'll see how Mark Dennehy took his belief system and turned Merrimack College into a vital, relevant entity again on and off the ice. There's so much more to explore within these pages, so I won't spoil any more here.

Each chapter of the book will be devoted to a coach and a specific topic, complete with a biography. The chapters consist of the transcribed interview that I had with each coach. At the end of each chapter, I'll weigh in with my feelings on each topic to close out the discussion. One final note about the chapters—some chapters will seem to be shorter than the others. This was done by design. I asked each coach the same number of questions, and some coaches were briefer in their responses. I left it this way to reflect the personality of each coach. For example, Merrimack's Mark Dennehy contains the longest interview in the book, and UMass Lowell's Norm Bazin has the shortest. Their responses are a reflection of their interview style, so I want to give the reader a sense of that. In chapter 13, I'll close the book by pulling the whole project together. So without any further ado, let's get right into it and drop the puck. I hope you enjoy reading this book as I enjoyed writing it.

C H A P T E R 1

Attitude

Nate Leaman, Providence College

Nate Leaman became the twelfth head coach in Providence College history on April 22, 2011. Coach Leaman arrived in Providence after coaching Union College for eight seasons, after posting a 138-127-35 mark at Union, becoming the winningest coach in school history. Nate led the Providence Friars to a 14-20-4 mark in 2011–2012, his first season in Providence, a season which saw the Friars qualify for the Hockey East tournament. The Friars defeated UMass Lowell in the quarterfinals before losing to eventual national champion Boston College at the TD Garden in Boston. In 2012–2013, he led the Friars to a berth in the in the Hockey East playoffs and a second consecutive trip to the Hockey East championship at TD Garden. In 2014–2015, Coach Leaman led the Friars to the school's first-ever national championship, defeating Boston University at TD Garden. His career has also seen him coach at Harvard under Mark Mazzoleni, and also as a volunteer coach for Shawn Walsh in Maine in 1998–99.

We open this volume with a discussion of attitude, one of the most fundamental building blocks of success. Any entity, whether it be a college hockey team, a manufacturing plant, or simply a person looking to achieve their goals in life, needs to understand the

1

importance of approaching his or her endeavors in life with a positive can-do attitude. This chapter will take a closer look at this concept. Stay with me at the end of the chapter for some closing thoughts on the subject.

> JL: So much of what we accomplish has to do with positive thinking and the proper mindset. Let's start with your general thinking on this concept based on your career as a whole. How do you approach your team on the importance of having a positive attitude throughout the long college hockey season?

> NL: I think you're exactly right. It's a long season for the kids, and you don't want to make the ups too high or the lows too far low, but in general just being optimistic and having a positive attitude. I think the more and more you find as a coach, that the more tension that guys carry, the more guys worry about things, the more that they have a generally a poor outlook; it really affects their energy level. It really affects their mental state. And it affects their ideals of success, in what they view they can accomplish. So having a positive attitude and coming to work every day—by work I mean practice or lifts every day—and just knowing that you're going to get better. I think that gives guys a real good positive attitude.

> JL: What do you feel is the most important ingredient in not only acquiring a positive attitude, but maintaining it over time?

> NL: I think looking at the big picture sometimes, when it's easy to look at the small

picture, having the long-term goals or the big frames in mind are important, and the big thing is just knowing you're not going to get anywhere with a bad attitude. You're just going to drain energy and have negative thoughts; it's just going to bring you backwards and drain teammates and drain other people around you. There's really no one that wants to be around a person that has a bad attitude, so just learning that having the big picture in mind, even if you're having a down day or some down times, that the sun's going to come up and just keep working and taking it one day at a time.

JL: If negativity does show itself in the locker room, how do you combat that as a head coach?

NL: I think you have to combat that right away. I'm usually more the type of guy that does it in front of the team because I know other guys see it. I'm a big believer in accountability, and I'm a big believer in that when you see those situations you attack them quickly, because if not, they can linger and then they can move away from the rink, and you never want that stuff to be away from the rink. You don't want it at the rink, but you certainly don't want it in a guy's dorm room late at night or around the dinner table or anything like that. So I think it's important that right away you're having conversations like "This is what you're portraying to us." A lot of times the individual doesn't understand what they're portraying to you, but this is what you're portraying to us and that's not acceptable—and we all need to be on the same page and move forward and to do that, I need you to be this way.

JL: What strategies do you use as a head coach to remain positive when things go badly, as they invariably do?

NL: I think you have to look at the big picture all the time, you have to know that each game is an individual event, each day is an individual event, and you can't live in the past. That's the thing about having a long season that I learn, more and more as you get older, is that you stop living in the past. When I was younger in my career, if we had a bad practice, I'd take it to bed at night, and I'd be so frustrated about it and so upset when I left the rink, and now sometimes you see that bad practice coming, and you find ways to make it a good practice, or you find ways to simplify the practice, but most importantly, tomorrow's another day. And you just keep focused on the future, keep focused on the bigger picture, even though you're taking it one day at a time, and I think that allows you to keep your focus and keep the right attitude.

JL: You recently completed your first season at Providence. It was, I'm sure, a learning experience for you and for the players to some extent. Do you feel that your positive approach rubbed off on them? How important is it as a leader to be enthusiastic and positive and to share that with your team?

NL: I think that the biggest thing is that the guys need to know that when they are coming down to the rink or in the weight room, they're getting better every day. And I think with that, in making sure they know that as a coaching staff and a strength staff that you're doing everything you can to help them, I think that really breeds a good attitude because they all want to get better. And then early in the season you're flowing in a lot of the team concepts, you're showing a lot of video clips of guys doing little things the right way, and I think that builds your team also and builds a better attitude. Overall, the guys know that what helps build a good attitude is that they're all accountable, and they know they're coming down to the rink to get better every day, and they know they have a coaching staff and a strength staff that's here to help them every day and really cares about them and everything they do every day. And with that, I think that's how you breed a great attitude. I don't think you can do that. I think it's something more about the culture that you have to set up, in them approaching things every day.

JL: Share with us a moment from 2011–12 with Providence that demonstrated a can-do, positive approach to winning hockey.

NL: I think probably the Merrimack weekend, actually. We came off a weekend sweep at Maine, we lost the first night in Maine in overtime, and the second game we lost in a real close game, we lost by a goal. I think we hit a post with the goalie pulled, it was just that close up in Maine. And after the second game, I said, "Hey, look, we got swept, it's something that none of us wanted, but the bottom line is it might make us better throughout the year, if we get to work." And if we understand that if we work this hard and we adjust a couple of things, I didn't think we were real good defensively in that series, but you know, we know we can get better. And I think that's the goal after every game—showing them what is the direction we need to go, what's the improvement we need to do. And you know, I didn't blow up at the guys after we got swept up in Maine, and the captains came up to me on the morning of the Monday after and just said, "We can't believe you didn't blow up." But the attitude was just we have to get better, and we have to learn from these situations. And the bottom line is, the other thing I said to them, was "Look, we lost in overtime, we missed an empty net in overtime, and lost the first night, and the second night we hit a post to tie it up late in a game." I told the guys, "Look these moments are going to even up throughout the year." So you have to keep them understanding and looking at the big picture and that's how you try to frame those things—you don't get too low in those bad situations. And then we come back a couple of weeks later, and we sweep Merrimack who was number one in the country at that time, and one of my captains came to me and said after that, "Do you have ESP?" And I didn't understand what they were saying at the time. I said I didn't even really get it, but then I learned what he was talking about; he was talking about how I told him that those overtime games and those close games even out, and we won a real close game with Merrimack, we won in overtime, and because of that, you get some believability from the guys in that looking at the big picture and just staying with the process one day at a time. Keep working and good things happen.

JL: One theory about behavior is that if you reinforce a behavior that you want to see repeated consistently, that behavior is likely to increase. Do the positive results a team gets serve as the biggest motivator to stay positive (i.e., such as a long winning streak)? That seems to be motivating in and of itself.

NL: Actually, no, a long winning streak is bad a lot of times. A long winning streak is actually one of the toughest things to do because there's complacency that settles in in those long winning streaks. As soon as you win three or four, then the guys start reading the press clippings, they start patting each other on the back too much. But it really takes a mature culture to stay in the process one day at a time, and I think overall, what breeds the good results is having a very

disciplined culture in that it's one day at a
time. We're working one day at a time; we're
not looking into the past, we're not looking too much in the present. We're going
to respect every opponent; we're going to
take things one day at a time and just try
to improve one day at a time. But there's no
doubt that positive results help to breed a
positive attitude. It's tough to have a positive
attitude when you're doing all those things
and you're not seeing the overall result. So
in those instances, as a coach, you have to
show them the little battles that you're winning; you know, guys doing the little things,
and reinforcing what you want in your culture. Showing video clips of a guy blocking
a shot, showing video clips of a guy finishing a hit, showing video clips of a guy catch-
ing a guy on a backcheck, little things that
you know are going to lead to the positive
results down the road, so those are ways to
keep it positive. But overall, certainly it's a
much better locker room to handle when
you're having positive results, but the long
winning streaks, for example, what BC did
this past year, is very, very difficult. You have
to credit Jerry York and the captains of their
team to what they did, because for complacency not to run in there it's really tough.

JL: Who would you describe as being the most
positive role model type player at PC and
why?

NL: I would say our captain this year was a pretty
positive guy, Danny New. Here's a guy that

a lot of players could talk with, a guy that obviously knew it was his last year of college hockey, so he was very enthused coming to the rink every day and knowing that it was his last crack, his last kick at the can, so he had a positive outlook. You know, he had some down games this year and always responded with a good game, so I think both those guys with their actions, with them coming to the rink every day and just busting their tails, I think that just kind of showed that, hey, I want to be here, I love being here, this is the best, and this is our last kick at the can, so let's have fun with this.

JL: How important is having a positive can-do attitude to you as a coach relative to other elements of success that are important to you?

NL: I think everything you do, you want to have a positive approach. You certainly don't want to go into anything with a negative approach even when there's negative times throughout the season. You want to go in and look at it like, "What's the situation here? "What's the big picture?" "Where do we need to get to here?" So now you can break it down and say although we are having some problems here, like maybe getting more fans in the stands, whether it be academics, or anything at the rink or away from the rink, you have to look at it as first, where do we want to get? Then, when we know where we want to go, now we can go break it down—where are we at, why are we there, and what are the steps we need to get there. So I think these are the types of things we try to focus on.

JL: Sum it up for us. What does having a positive attitude mean to Nate Leaman both personally and professionally?

NL: Having fun every day and loving what you're doing. As I mentioned previously, lay it all on the line every day and try to give your best every day, so at the end of the day, the players walk away from the program, and they know they don't have one regret. They know the staff worked extremely hard to make them better people and making them better ice hockey players, and overall trying to make Providence College and the tradition of the program and everyone who wears the jersey proud of that. So having a positive attitude and having a lot of pride in what you're doing, and knowing that every day you're doing your best to make everyone around you better, and make it an enjoyable experience.

Closing Thoughts on Attitude

Your attitude determines your altitude in life. The questions you ask yourself determine the results you are going to get. The self-help author Tony Robbins states that "Quality questions create a quality life." Are you asking questions of power or of limitation? If you can approach every situation in your life with enthusiasm and a can-do spirit of achievement, the results will transcend your expectations. Attitudes are also contagious, and they can spread like wildfire, whether they be positive or negative. As Coach Leaman alluded to earlier, what kind of culture are you committed to being a part of? An environment of growth or negativity?

Let me illustrate a few examples of attitude in action. I go to the gym regularly, and while I am there, I run into a man who is probably in his late fifties to early sixties. He is a regular there, and he is limited by some physical and mobility issues. His neck is permanently crooked to one side and his speech is affected. I have many people who complain about going to the gym and working out, but this man is not one of them. Every day I see him working out, squatting and thrusting on the machines. He lies on the incline bench and does sit-ups, completely oblivious to the limitations that he has. And he always approaches each day and each workout with a smile, never feeling sorry for himself. Aside from being a joy to be around, he truly is an inspiration because of his infectious, positive attitude. I always think, "If this man can work out with his current physical limitations and enjoy it, what does that say about me and my workout and what I can accomplish?"

Travis Roy was another example of a man who demonstrated an incredible positive approach to life. Being dealt a horrible circumstance in life—seeing his college hockey career end just eleven seconds after it started at BU and becoming a quadriplegic—would be enough to cause anyone to get down on themselves and feel sorry for themselves. But not Travis. He rose above that and was a beacon for inspiring others through his work following the injury. I had the great fortune of meeting Travis years ago and again at the Hockey East championships in 2013 and was immediately touched and impressed by his genuine positive attitude toward life.

I also believe that having a positive approach is manifested in college hockey—and all athletics for that matter—by noticing the behavior of a team when they are at their darkest hour. The outlook a team has when they are on the edge of defeat can speak volumes about how the results will turn out. You see it all the time—teams come back from nearly improbable odds to win a game or a championship because they kept it positive. They saw adversity as their ally and made it work for them. BU experienced that in 2009 when they rallied to defeat Miami to win the national championship in over-time after being down 3-1 with a minute left in regulation. No player on that bench thought that BU would lose; although good fortune played a role, as you will hear later from Jack Parker. BU won the game and the national title because of their winning, positive never-say-die approach.

Surround yourself with people of enthusiasm, encouragement, and positivity. Make sure your support system is that of a positive nature, and you'll be climbing the ladder of success just like the Providence Friars did in 2014–2015, winning the national championship in Division 1 men's college hockey.

CHAPTER 2

Overcoming Adversity

Kevin Sneddon, University of Vermont

Kevin Sneddon is entering his eleventh season at the helm of Vermont hockey in 2013–14. He led the Catamounts to consecutive NCAA tournament appearances, including a spot in the Frozen Four in Washington, DC, in 2009. He was named the Bob Kullen, Hockey East Coach of the Year (2007–08) and has also been a finalist for National Coach of the Year in the same season. A 1992 graduate of Harvard University, he is just the third head coach in the past forty-four years at Vermont. He also saw time with the Los Angeles Kings of the NHL.

The second chapter is devoted to a subject we all will deal with in our lifetimes—overcoming adversity. No matter what walk of life you come from, there will be pratfalls. The extent to which you manage these obstacles will define who you become. It is not the events that occur in our lives that are significant, but how we choose to deal with them that shapes who we ultimately become. Guiding us through this chapter is Kevin Sneddon, the bench boss at the University of Vermont. The 2011–12 season was a difficult one for the Vermont Catamounts—Coach Sneddon's squad posted just three league victories in twenty-seven games, going 3-23-1, while finishing with a 6-27-1 record for the season. Kevin will give us his thoughts on how to approach the difficult challenges that adversity presents, and I'll close with my final thoughts at the end of the chapter.

> JL: Whatever the endeavor in life, obstacles and adversity are bound to show up in life at some point. What is your personal philosophy about overcoming adversity?

> KS: Well, I think my personal philosophy is, you need it. You know, you have to have adversity in order to understand your limitations, and I think through adversity you grow as a person, certainly as an individual, and within our sport and within life in general. Again, it shows you what you need to work on, things you need to get better at. I think it's very humbling—I think it allows you the opportunity to reflect on the support systems you have around you, whether it's family or whether it's friendships. All those things through adversity really pull together and help you through tough times, and as I said, I think it's a necessary evil in life. When you're going through it, it's not always that fun, but I think when you're able to get through it, the sense of accomplishment and the sense of growth really does help you out.

> JL: Last season, the Catamounts struggled in the standings in spite of a consistent nightly disciplined effort on the ice. What was your message to the team during those times in an attempt to keep things positive as you strived to get better?

KS: Well, again, that was probably the biggest thing, trying to find a way to stay positive. You know, when we had so many injuries, it was very difficult to get on the bus for a road trip and leave behind six or seven of our better players, and you know, to have a team that felt confident that we could win without those guys was a daunting task. But again, I think for us, it was all about pride. This program has had some great moments over the last three or four years, and I think our guys naturally have felt a sense of disappointment that they were letting people down. And what we tried to reflect on was just that we can't control that—you know, we can't control the injuries, we can't control some of the other issues we were faced with off the ice. What we can control is how we try to dominate the day. That's something that we talk a lot about, especially now in the offseason here. It's just that you try to focus on what you can control—you can't control the losses that have already happened, you can't worry about the future. You have to go out there and play as hard as you can. And play for pride. I think that's one thing that we talked about right to the final buzzer of our last game against Boston College was that nobody can take away the pride unless we let them.

JL: One of the more common beliefs about adversity can be thought of as "what doesn't kill you makes you stronger." Do you agree with that statement, and if so, how true is that statement for you?

KS: As alluded to earlier, I think that statement is very, very true. Again, it's very difficult to go through things in your life that at the time feel like they're the most difficult obstacle to overcome, but once you get through it, and you grow from it, it's a very rewarding process. In the sport of ice hockey, it's very difficult because you are dealing with emotions of probably—you know I can't just count the twenty-eight players because you have an entire staff—there's more than thirty-some odd people that are affected by the adversity, and to try and get everybody to get through it at the same time is certainly very difficult. Personally, I have always felt that it makes you a stronger person. And it's definitely necessary in life. I think it gives you a healthy perspective on things, through ice hockey in particular, that somebody's always worse off than you are, and the advice my parents always gave me was that no matter how hard you think you have it, you're not off defending the country somewhere, or you have your health. There's always a way to look at things in a more positive light while you're going through that adversity.

JL: Share a moment in your career in Vermont which provides an example of adversity being overcome in action.

KS: Well, this is probably a good year to reflect back on; the fact that our guys, I felt at least, played very well disciplined, played very determined, right through to the final buzzer. You know, you look at what the media was saying about us, what our own fans were saying about us, what we were probably saying in our own minds about each other, I think that's living proof. I think we'll be able to have this conversation next year—you know, at the end of next year—and say this was a great example of a team going through some adversity, so you know, we face it every year. Whether we made the Frozen Four, whether you make the NCAA tournament, or you win the Hockey East championship, teams go through adversity all the time, and again, going back to it, it is necessary for a team to win a championship. Now that adversity might be minor compared to something like what we went through this year, but I think if you talk to Jerry York about his championship run this year, going through the goaltending issues they went through this year probably made their team stronger in the long run. It certainly made Parker Milner strong in the long run, so again, I'm a big fan of adversity from the standpoint of I think you need it to become your best.

JL: From your personal perspective, what do you feel is that most important psychological mindset to have in tackling adversity?

KS: Dominate the day. Again, I don't mean to be repetitive, but there's nothing you can do about yesterday, there's nothing we can do about tomorrow, and you have to focus on today and what can you do today to try and be better. And if you can get a team focused on that, that's a very difficult mental task. We've probably worked the most on that over the past seven months. It's just let's put away the past, we can't do anything about that; we can't go back and play those games over, and we sure as heck can't start tackling our schedule now. What we can do is focus on things that can make us better today. Control the controllables and get rid of everything else.

JL: Both in general and referring back to last season, how big a role does your team captains play in helping to spread your message about working hard and battling when things don't go your way?

KS: Well, your leaders are a direct descendent from your coaching staff, so you know, again, I have taken full blame for this past season and not being able to have our guys enjoy the process a little bit more. I think we got wrapped up in the emotion of it at times, but your captains have to be on the same page as the coaching staff. Their message has to be different to the team, but we place a ton of value on your leaders. We like to have representatives in every class. We try to meet at least on a biweekly basis just to make sure that we tackle any small issues out there. We often refer to the "broken window" theory that we've got to fix things before they get further damaged. But your leaders are everything in college hockey, because quite frankly we're only around the team two hours a day; the captains are around the rest of the guys far more than we are, and I think it's pivotal. I've been blessed to have some great leaders here at the University of Vermont, and we have one now that's going to take us in the right direction in H. T. Lenz.

JL: A few of your colleagues here in Hockey East are of the opinion that one should never let the emotional highs get too high and the lows get too low during the course of a long college hockey season. How much truth is there in that statement for you, and if so, how important is that principle to manage adversity when it arises?

KS: Well, it is. It is a long season. College hockey is longer than any season out there, and I've often said that nowadays we put so much pressure on ourselves as coaches, that often times the wins you don't get to enjoy because you're hungry for the next one, and losses you tend to eat for too long. And if a coach can flip that around a little bit and learn to enjoy the wins a little more without getting too high, and make sure the losses don't consume you, kind of flush it down the toilet as quickly as possible, those are the guys that are going to stay in this business the longest. The guys like Jack Parker, you know, he's got a lot of wins, but he's also had some tough losses, and I think the quicker you can put away the losses, and at the same time enjoy the wins, while maintaining the not getting too high or too low, our job as coaches is to keep the guys even keeled. Keep them focused and keep pushing them.

Whether it's a great win or a tough loss, hey, it's turn the next page.

JL: When it comes to overcoming obstacles, who do you feel is the most inspirational individual you have encountered while dealing with troubles and why, either hockey related or personally?

KS: You know, I gain inspiration from a lot of different people. Usually it's from my players; maybe it's watching a guy overcome a really bad injury. You know, we've had guys here like Matt Hansen who was paralyzed on the ice. We've had a number of different guys go through some really tough family ordeals, so I think for me it's all about picking different inspirations from different people. The other day Mike Paliotta got up in front of the team in an emotional way and talked about one of his inspirations being his mom, battling and beating breast cancer and how positive she was during this whole thing, so there's stories all around us, and I just try to eat it up as much as I can. Off the top of my head. I can't think of one person, but certainly my parents. My mom and dad separated early on when I was young, and to look at how my mom was able to handle that adversity and still allow me to play the sport that I love, I still don't know how she managed to work a full-time job and get me to the hockey rink all the time and take care of my younger sister. Again, there's inspiration in overcoming adversity everywhere we turn, we just to have notice it.

JL: What lessons did in dealing with last year's struggles do you feel Vermont gained as a team? And more importantly, how much do you feel it will be a motivating factor going forward?

KS: I think the biggest lesson that we learned is that what's more important than x's and o's is our team culture, and the emphasis on our core values. So for us, this last seven weeks has been all about building the team back together, committing to a new set of core values that everybody is buying into, and that's pride, selflessness, and toughness, in everything we do. Whether it's out in the community, in the classroom, in the weight room, or on the ice, those are the three values of what it means to be a Catamount hockey player. As difficult as it was to go through, I think it's going to be a huge positive in the long run, because that was a great reminder that it's not about x's and o's, and it's not about power plays; sure those things count, but it's really all about a group of twenty-eight guys going in the right direction, and Merrimack is a great example of that. Mark Dennehy has done a wonderful job of getting guys to buy into a culture and playing for each other and playing for the school, having that pride, going out there, and leaving it all out there every time they put that jersey on, whether it's for practice or for games. And we got away from that a little bit, and that's my job to get us back on track.

JL: Lastly, in summation, Kevin, what is your personal advice on how best to overcome adversity for those in any walk of life?

KS: The best advice I can give is to utilize the people around you. I think sometimes when we go through adversity, we go into a shell. And it's okay to need help, it's okay to rely on others. It doesn't mean it's a weakness; if anything I think it's a sign of strength. Most people are surrounded by friends and family, and those are the people that are going to get you through the times, and as long as you don't shut the door on that, you can get through anything. And if people go into the mindset that adversity isn't necessarily a bad thing, it's a much healthier way to look at things.

Closing Thoughts on Overcoming Adversity

Adversity is something we will all face. It takes the form of many different shapes and sizes. I truly believe that what happens to you is not as important as how you process it and deal with it. A perfect example of this is the story of a cousin of mine, a very close cousin, who suffered a debilitating injury many years ago in California. He was the victim of a gunshot wound that left him paralyzed and with a spinal cord injury. This cousin of mine was always independent and self-reliant prior to his injury, and his new circumstances in life truly put a crimp in his usual manner of doing things. As I alluded to in the chapter on attitude, this man could have easily packed it in and let the adversity consume him, but he chose to focus on what he could control and how best to achieve living as productive a life as he could. I remember grabbing his hands and helping him manage flights of stairs. I also recall watching him dive into a swimming pool despite his injuries. He was unstoppable because he asked himself empowering questions designed to help him thrive, choosing not to feel sorry for himself and letting his adversity get the better of him.

In college hockey circles, I only need to remember my early years of calling hockey games at Merrimack to get an understanding of adversity in action. Mark Dennehy took the reins at Merrimack the same time I got there, and the team struggled mightily for the first few years. In fact the team hit its nadir in the 2006–07 season, winning just three games. In spite of the nightly effort, sweat, and toil, the wins were not coming. But Coach Dennehy never allowed the team, himself, or anyone else associated with the program to get caught up in the lack of success in the win column. He took the adversity the team was experiencing on the ice and turned it into a positive. The focus was always on if you work hard enough, long enough, good things will happen. Can we say now that Merrimack has prospered since dealing with that adversity? I think so. I think back to the 2010–11 season, where Merrimack faced Boston College at TD Garden for the Hockey East championship, and then squaring off against Notre Dame in the NCAA regionals in Manchester, New Hampshire, for an opportunity to face UNH for a berth in the Frozen Four. Adversity can help you grow if you take the opportunity to learn from it and have the patience to see it through.

Adversity will occur in our lives. We can't control the events that happen to us, but we can control our responses to them. I believe that two things are important in managing adversity, and Coach Sneddon addressed both of them—focus on the present moment and engage your support system. Never feel like you are alone in dealing with trouble, because in reality, there is someone in your life that has gone through something similar, and they can be a source of great strength. And when things are going badly and adverse situations are engulfing you, it is so easy to flood your mind with thoughts of despair, mulling over the past and being concerned about the future. Try to remember that the present is the only reality you can live in. Stay grounded and focus on the present moment. Coach Sneddon and the Catamounts dominate their days during practice, and you can do the same.

Commitment to Excellence

Jim Madigan, Northeastern University

Jim Madigan entered this third year behind the Northeastern Huskies bench in 2013–14, after guiding the team to a 13-16-5 mark in 2011–12 and to a record of 9-21-4 in 2012–13. A graduate of Northeastern, he is a three-time Beanpot champion and just the tenth coach in the program's storied history. Coach Madigan played for the Huskies from 1981 to 1985 and also served as the team's assistant coach from 1986 to 1993. He has also served as a scout with the New York Islanders and Pittsburgh Penguins organizations, winning a Stanley Cup ring in 2009 with Pittsburgh. He has also served as an assistant coach at the University of Vermont. He also was the recipient of the Fern C. Flaman award in 1998 for his outstanding service to NU hockey.

We now move on to the subject of commitment—more specifically the commitment to excellence. We all strive to be great and to have the inner drive to finish first in everything we do. We are a competitive society! However, it is not an easy process. Being a winner and committing to success is easier said than done. Do you have what it takes to commit, to truly commit to achieving the results you want? I'd like to introduce you now to Jim Madigan, the head coach at Northeastern University, who will share his opinions on how he gets Northeastern University to believe in the commitment to excellence. Stick around at the end of this chapter, and I'll give you my thoughts on this all-important topic to wrap things up.

> JL: When it comes to Northeastern hockey, from your perspective, how do you, as Coach Madigan, define total commitment to the program's success? What does it mean to you?

> JM: From our perspective, it's making sure that when we bring student athletes in here, we've got players who understand the word *commitment*, and what we're trying to do here to create a winning program to create that winning culture, is to create that commitment to excellence. Commitment to excellence for us means that you've got to be excellent at doing all the right things in every aspect of your life. It's just not like a faucet where you can turn it on and be like, "Okay, I'm going to be good in practice, but later I'm not going to go to my class, I'm not going to put the work ethic into getting good grades, I'm going to leave another component of my life to the side." Commitment to excellence is doing all the right things in every aspect of your life on a consistent basis. So it becomes secondhand, second nature. You're not thinking about what you need to do to be successful. At the end of the day we all want to be successful in whatever we choose to do, but you've got to lead your life in such a way that you're

able to sustain it, and you're able to maintain a certain level of excellence. And here, if you want to be an elite athlete, it means you've got to be doing all the right things in the classroom, all the right things in the weight room, all the right things on the ice, and making sure you get the proper rest and diet and everything off the ice it takes to be a committed athlete. There's a commitment that goes with excellence, and if you're not willing to make that commitment, then excellence won't follow. So it's leading your life in doing all the right things in every aspect of your life, so that you can attain, and then maintain, excellence.

JL: Commitment is often associated with sacrifice; we often hear those two words together. What types of sacrifices do you feel are common to a college hockey player to achieve success?

JM: From a sacrifice perspective, student athletes are unique people on a college campus. College kids come to Northeastern, or any other university, and they want to enjoy the academics, they want to enjoy the social components, the friendships, the relationships, and all that. And certainly with our student athletes, we want them to come in and make a commitment to be academic first and foremost, to the athletics, and we want them to have them to have relationship and social opportunities. But the sacrifice that they're going to have to have to make, that when kids are going out Friday and Saturday nights, or during the week and having fun, the student athlete has to maintain a discipline to their regimen. And they are in a regimen Monday through Sunday, and there's a sacrifice that goes with that. You are different. God gave you a talent, and you have now taken that talent and tried to refine it and be the best you can be and putting in all the hard work and sacrifice—sacrifice in the weight room, sacrifice in practice, (before, during, and after practice), sacrifice from the mental component of the game and preparation. So you put in all that time and all that commitment and want to make sure that always gets funneled in the right direction—so sacrifices are the friendships, the friendships that most college kids have. You have them, but maybe in a more moderate area, where you can't go out every Friday night, you've got to prepare for that weekend series, etc. This is a full-time job for student athletes, school and hockey, so they have to make sure that they're always preparing themselves for being the best they can be when that time comes where it's time for them to perform. So they're making a commitment when they're coming here to making sure they're doing all the right things in order for them to be able to perform at their highest and greatest level.

JL: You recently completed your first season here at Northeastern. What was your message to the team when you first arrived about the importance of committing to the type of culture you wanted here?

JM: Culture is a big word here that we use, and we have a culture that we want to achieve here and maintain and sustain throughout the course of the year, and so we built a culture based on our foundational keys, which are based on competitiveness, work ethic, accountability, and passion. And it was important for us in developing that culture that everything we do centers around those four themes and those foundational keys. And those are going to be the keys to our success moving forward here at Northeastern. And those four keys, competitiveness, work ethic, passion, accountability, we want to make sure all our student athletes have it not just here at the ice rink, but as I said earlier, they have to have a commitment in every aspect of their life, because they are interrelated. If you're not committed, or putting in 100 percent forth in hockey, then it's going to affect your academics. If you're not doing the right thing academically, then it's going to affect your hockey, or it's going to affect your relationships or other areas of your life. So for us, it was important for us that we establish the right culture, because the culture was going to allow us to maintain the commitment toward excellence that we want to have in order for our team to be successful. You have to have a culture, and part of that culture, is, obviously, a winning culture and a commitment to excellence, but you need to establish the foundational keys that are going to help drive you and be the vehicle to get you to that commitment to excellence.

JL: If you could name only one player, who do you feel demonstrated a prototypical commitment to success from last year's Northeastern squad and why?

JM: Commitment to excellence for me from the 2011–12 team would have to be our captain, Michael McLaughlin. Michael McLaughlin is the type of person that, every time he comes to the rink, he's giving you 100 percent of his time, of his talent, and of his commitment to doing the right thing. He's the hardest worker in practice; his attention to detail, doing the drills the right way, practicing hard, making sure his teammates get better each and every day. His work ethic and his ability to be infectious in creating a positive atmosphere with our team, with his teammates, so that he's leading by example on the ice, helping to create that culture of winning when we're on the ice at practice. And then what you look for as he carries that forward, the games become second nature to him, because he's done it in practice all week long. But more than just being at practice, he was a 4.0 student this year. He's a 3.6 student overall. He's led it, and he does it by example each and every day in each and every aspect of his life, from the classroom to the hockey, to the community. He has worked with local schools and reading. He mentors on campus, and he's a student advisor on campus. So Michael McLaughlin's approach to life is, I'm going to do everything the right way, I'm going to work the hardest I can, I'm going to get the most out of my talent, and I'm never going to be cheated. I'm always going to be happy with the effort that I can put forth. It might not always get me the net results, but I'm never going to walk away from the rink knowing that I didn't give 100 percent of my time and a commitment to succeeding and toward excellence.

JL: If commitment waivers, for whatever reason, what do you communicate as a coach to get things back on track?

JM: Commitment does waver. You have to ask the players to use the mirror test—to look into a mirror and say, "Can you honestly look into that mirror and say that you're 100 percent committed in making the right sacrifices for you as a player and an individual, and for you as part of a larger concept as being part of the team?" And the mirror test, if you're honest with yourself, it's going to give you the result or an answer that you might not be happy with. So commitment all falls to the individual. We coaches push our players—and all college coaches are doing that regardless of the sport—and preach about culture and commitment and about winning and about doing all the right things, but the individual has to adopt that in their normal everyday life. So how do you get back on track when they're wavering? You try and have that honest conversation—the mirror test—and then you try to give them examples on how they can bring it back to the commitment they need to have. Because at times players will think they're giving you 100 percent of their commitment when they're actually not. And so you just have to be honest with them when they're not making that commitment, and then create an opportunity for them to understand what that commitment actually is and continue to drive them toward that. You normally see it when players come in as first-year students, and because they have not been part of a culture, like as in college athletics, you're trying for them to show them that commitment, and you're trying to have them take a look at some of the older guys—the senior leadership, the veteran leadership, who are committed—and they can learn from those veterans in all aspects, whether it be on the ice or off the ice. So that's another opportunity where you're trying to have the players, if they have veered away from that total commitment, for them to take a look at some of the kids who do have that 100-percent commitment, and then you're giving them examples of how they can get back on track.

JL: How closely is pride in your hockey program related to commitment to excellence?

JM: They are tied together, 100 percent, very much so, in the sense that you want to be proud to be a Northeastern player, and you need to have pride in everything that you do. Pride and commitment go hand in hand. You should be proud of the fact that you want to be the best you can be. And that's an inner drive—a drive that comes from within. And it comes from wanting to have excellence; you want to win, and how are you going to get there? And pride plays a big part in how you're going to develop that commitment. You want to be better than your teammate that's sitting beside you, you want to be better than your opponent you're playing against. You want to be the best you can be, and pride is the driver of that type of success. So they are related to us. We talk an awful lot here bout culture, and about commitment, also about pride, and about being here at Northeastern University, and that you're fortunate to be here at Northeastern, that we've selected you, and Northeastern's fortunate to have you to be part of the program because of the aspects or characteristics that you bring to our institution, but pride is a big driver of that commitment.

JL: Connected to the concept of pride, have you had the opportunity to draw on the experiences from the history of Northeastern hockey, and it is quite a rich program, to reinforce your message about commitment to excellence? If so, can you share an example?

JM: We are always bringing examples. I am, and I'm, fortunate enough to have enough history with the program going back twenty-five plus years about people who have laid down some of the groundwork here for our current players, and who have helped lay down a foundation, in that it's allowing our players to continue to build on it. Northeastern's got a rich tradition of hockey players. Certainly we have excellence, and we strive for more excellence from our players and our program, and we want to be able to continue to build on the future of what Northeastern's players have built on, but also to be able to create their own mark and leave their own fingerprints on this program. And if I were to draw back on some moments of pride that we try and drive from, quite frankly it's some of the winning teams that have had success here at Northeastern. And it's not individuals, but it's built on team success. And the teams that have won here have been teams that might not have had the most talent, might not have had the top recruit, we might not have had the bells and whistles that some other programs might have had at that time of competition going back over the years, but they were hard workers. They were overachievers and they bonded together as a team. They came together for a common goal, and they had a mindset that they were not going to be denied. They had a work ethic that said, "We're going to outwork other talented teams." We had talent, and we had players in every position, but it was the sum of the parts that allowed us to be successful. So those moments of pride, and I've been fortunate to be able to be a player on some of those teams, or coaching some of those teams, that we've used to try and motivate some of our players, and highlighting and illustrating some of the teams that because of their work ethic, because of their commitment, and because of some of the pride they've demonstrated each and every day moving through the season, that's going to allow us to have success, and show that vision of success and what it looks like so that we can replicate that for our team moving forward.

JL: This can be thought of as a hockey question, or a question in general terms: how big a role does mastering fundamentals have in achieving excellence?

JM: It plays a key role. It's the foundation, for me, to our success, and to any team's success, in that you have to be fundamentally sound in order to have success. Winning a game, or winning a championship at the end of the year, people always say, take care of the little things and the big things will take care of themselves. The little things are the fundamental aspects of hockey. You've got to have the basic foundations down, you've got to all be on the same page, you've got to be willing to sacrifice and do the little things right. If you do the little things right, all these small little pieces will accumulate into success, whether it be during the course of a game or during the course of a season. Fundamentally, it's on ice. It also lends itself to off ice—it's the proper sleep, the proper diet, taking care of yourself during a long-extended season. There are core fundamental aspects that you believe in and what you try to live during the course of the year, and if you don't waver from that core, from that foundation, or from those fundamentals, you're going to be successful at the end of the year. But we're always talking here about the fundamentals, let's do all the little things well and let's be fundamentally sound. And if we're fundamentally sound, then that will take care of the larger things. It plays a key role and is a foundation for your success moving forward.

JL: Are there any specific hockey players from your coaching experience that illustrate the commitment to excellence to excellence more than others?

JM: I was fortunate to work in the Pittsburgh Penguins organization for five years, and I don't think you have to look any farther than number 87, Sidney Crosby. He brings it every single day of his life. He is as committed on the ice as he is off the ice. His preparation is second to none, and he doesn't leave any stone unturned in how he trains. His training regimen represents and reflects what he does on the ice, and on the ice, he's driven to be the best he can be. Every single day he wants to be the best. If he wasn't playing hockey, if he was a doctor or an attorney, he'd be the best in those two professions. He's got a commitment level that's second to none, and he's got a burning desire to not only be the best player he can be, but to make the players around him be the best they can be. So he takes it upon himself. He knows he's got a great talent, and he knows he's got to work at it, but he knows that "for us to be successful, it's important that the other twenty guys as a team be successful for us to win a championship." And so, he takes it upon himself and assumes that mantle to make everyone else around him better. He has helped fuel some of the other great players on that Penguins team, one other being Evgeni Malkin, who is a great talent. And for Malkin to watch Crosby practice every day, work hard in everything he does, has made Geno Malkin a greater player than what he was when he came in five or six years ago. So for me it's the great ones: 99, 66, and 87. Crosby, I think, in hockey reflects the most committed player to excellence in our sport right now.

JL: Lastly, Coach, let's sum this up. In terms of your personal philosophy about commitment to excellence, what strategies would you advise to people who want to master this all-important trait?

JM: It goes back to what I said earlier. If you're committed to excellence, then you've got to be committed in every area of your life. We've talked about just the student's athlete's life, in that being the three components that are most important to him or her while they are here on a college campus—academics, athletics, and social opportunities and community. If you're committed, you're all in—not in just one component of your life, but in all three parts of your life. And then if you walk away, you go outside of the regular student-athlete. For example, if I look at Jim Madigan's commitment to excellence, it's being a good father and being a good husband, it's being involved in the community and giving back where I can give back. It's professionally doing the best you can do every day you come to work, and try to have excellence, in effect, not only in your job but also the people that you work with and helping them out to be the best they can be. So you're all in. It's a philosophy for me in that if you're committed to excellence, someone should be able to look from afar and see Jim Madigan and see it in anything I do and that's what we try and preach to our players—that's my philosophy, in that in order for commitment to excellence to happen, it's got to happen in all the areas of your life, and if you do that, and do all the right things, then you'll never stray from that line of commitment to excellence. You might not always win, you might not always get that net result, but you're never going to walk away feeling that you didn't give 100 percent, feeling that you didn't do everything in your power to be able to achieve success, then that in itself is reaching success because you're only going to walk away happy with your effort and happy with the accomplishments because you've done everything in your possible power to be the best.

Closing Thoughts on Commitment to Excellence

Committing to excellence starts with mastering the fundamentals and setting a personal standard regarding your code of conduct—a code which indicates clearly what you are committed to achieving and also what you are not willing to accept or tolerate. Oftentimes in life, it is the little things that matter most, and stacking multiple little things on top of each other can create a wildfire of success that rages like a forest fire.

One of my favorite examples in talking about commitment to excellence comes from my time in baseball. From 2005 to 2007, I worked for a minor league team in Lynn, Massachusetts, called the North Shore Spirit. They were an independent team who were owned and operated by a man named Nick Lopardo. A man who was very successful in business, Nick decided to branch out and take steps toward his vision of owning a sports team. He bought the Spirit and relocated them from Waterbury, Connecticut, to Lynn. From day one, this was a man whose drive to be the best became his all-consuming passion. His commitment to excellence was unlike anything I had ever experienced. He would focus on every detail—it was once speculated that Nick could see every scrap of paper inside the stadium. He treated every aspect of the organization with a painstaking commitment to excellence. He would even clean toilets and power wash the seating area himself, and he proudly would proclaim that his ballpark, Fraser Field, was the "cleanest ballpark in America." We as his employees were never allowed to take shortcuts. Nick pushed us to all be better because those are the standards he lived by, and in his view, anyone who worked for him needed to embrace that philosophy in their can-approach to the Spirit, or we would not be his employees for long.

Mike Machnik is my color analyst at Merrimack, and I've never been around a person who is more passionate and more committed to college hockey than him. Mike is like a sponge; he has a burning desire to absorb every bit of knowledge that he can, whether it be by talking to people or the amount of preparation and research that he does prior to a game. He is a man who is committed to the success of the broadcast and to the process of promoting college hockey at Merrimack. Mike illustrates what Coach Madigan talked about in terms of doing all the little things right and setting your standards in such a way as to achieve excellence.

Commitment to excellence is all encompassing. Wanting to excel is good. Desiring to excel is great. But do you have what it takes to really commit to that goal of yours every step of the way? Committing to excel means first deciding to do it. It all starts with a decision, a decision that will young be denied. It means that no other option besides being victorious will be accepted, no matter what obstacles you may need to overcome. From my own life, I have lost over fifty pounds (and still dropping) after facing a weight problem head on. How did I do it? Once I got some potentially bad news from my doctor, I committed right then and there that I was committed to getting healthy, getting in shape, and doing all the right things not once in a while, but every day. Exercise and a good diet became a must, a top priority. Today I visit the gym six days a week and drink a gallon of water every day, religiously. I don't say these things to impress you, but only to impress upon you what can be done when you truly commit to success.

Coach Madigan also talks about sacrifice, and the truly great are willing to put in the time, effort, and sacrifice in to be the greatest of the great. It may mean staying after hours after everyone has gone home. It means going the extra mile. No matter what business you find yourself in in life, the ones that succeed are the ones that give just that little extra, just that much more than their competition lives. It might mean doing one extra crunch at the gym, it might mean calling home when you're on the road to tell your family you love them, or any other behavior that shows you're truly committed to what you're doing. In hockey, it might mean sacrificing your body to block a shot. If you can keep your goal in sight and are willing to do anything to make it materialize, not only can you then say that you are truly committed, but that excellence and victory will then follow.

CHAPTER 4

Belief

Mark Dennehy, Merrimack College

Mark Dennehy is entering his ninth season behind the Merrimack bench in 2013–2014. He is the architect behind the complete rebuilding and flourishing of the hockey program at Merrimack College. Under Coach Dennehy's leadership, Merrimack set a Division 1 school record with twenty-five wins in 2010–2011 while reaching the NCAA tournament for the first time since 1988 and also reaching the Hockey East Championship for the first time in school history. In 2011–2012, Merrimack reached the number 1 status nationally for the first time ever. He was named the 2009–2010 and 2010–2011 All New England Coach of the Year and was Co-Coach of the Year in Hockey East in 2009–2010.

There may be no better person to talk about the subject of belief in Hockey East than a man who has believed in his program from day one: Mark Dennehy of Merrimack College. Coach Dennehy came to North Andover with a plan and a vision and patiently endured some very difficult times before helping to turn the hockey program into not only a respected entity in Hockey East, but a team of national recognition. This chapter will talk about belief—that source of certainty that fuels us and propels us to achieve results beyond our wildest hopes and expectations. Enjoy these golden nuggets from Coach

Dennehy and then I'll be back at the end of the chapter to wrap things up with my thoughts.

> JL: Eight years ago, you came on the scene here at Merrimack College. The culture back was a lot different back then than where it is now. What comprised your belief system in terms of your vision for the program when you took the job back then, and do you feel like that vision has materialized?

> MD: It's a constant—I don't want to say struggle, but you're constantly cultivating it, that belief system. And it's very fragile. The more success you have, the stronger that belief system gets. But if you fail with consistency, it can fracture in a hurry. It's really all about controlling what you can control and setting a standard. And when I say controlling what you can control, it's your work ethic, your decision making away from the rink, discipline, perseverance. Those are the things that I think really help to form a belief. And it's not something that happens overnight, so there needs to be a level of patience. But it's like everything else—it takes a long time to cultivate, and a short amount of time to disintegrate, so we're constantly vigilant.

> JL: How would you summarize your techniques or belief system that you have here in place at Merrimack as it relates to your personal philosophies?

> MD: I don't know how much they are my techniques. I think most of the stuff we all do

is somewhat borrowed. You may add your own flavor to it, but those are things that I learned through life, and through coaching with some great coaches, the likes of Don Cahoon, Bill Gilligan, Jimmy Stewart, right on down the line. It really began and ended with hard work. Hard work started with me, assistant coaches, and making sure that there's a standard that we meet, and then every player you bring in, there being an understanding that we're going to attempt to outwork our opponents. That's really the beginning of it. The analogy I give is you wake up in the morning and you commit to being the best student athlete, father, or hockey coach you can be. You do as much in that day as you can, and then before you go to bed, you look back in the mirror and evaluate yourself, and you have to be honest with yourself. And you're not going to bat a thousand, you're not going to be 100 percent, but it's about being honest and doing the same thing, and if you do that enough over a long period of time, then there is a belief system that will take hold.

JL: What has been your experience in how best to convert a belief into a conviction?

MD: I think they're almost one in the same. If you do believe in what you're doing, then there will be a conviction in your play, or in your ability to do things. If you look at conviction and belief they really are abstract notions, and I think it's important to bring it back to reality, and that's why you want to concentrate on the things that you can control, so if you just concentrate on "Hey, guys, we've got to believe" or "We've got to play with conviction," no, we want to substantiate it. We want to give it some substance. We want to work hard; we want to play fast. I want student athletes that are interested in getting an education and that are going to get up and go to class even when it's rainy, snowy, or whatever. If you live that day to day, then this abstract notion of belief, or conviction, becomes tangible. So for us, it's really about trying to bring it down to ground level.

JL: When you are implementing a strategy which is consistent with a belief system, how important is it to be flexible in your approach? Is there an example of a time when you changed something to achieve a more desired result with Merrimack?

MD: Well, I'm of the volition that I didn't invent the game, and I may not be the smartest guy, but I've surrounded myself with good people, and I've got a lot of resources that we can go to. I want our guys to be prepared. There is one example I can think of, and it goes hand in hand with the type of empowered environment that we've tried to create here, where the players really feel like they're a part of it, they're a part of everything. We were playing against Maine in the playoffs a couple of years ago, and we had two different ways that we could forecheck. We work on both ways, and there are reasons or rationales for either, and we started out the first game of the playoff series forechecking a certain way. They had a lot of success coming out, we really weren't that effective on the forecheck for whatever reason, and I don't know exactly that there was only one reason. And as the head coach I'm pondering, "Is it time to make a change? Do we want to go to the second forecheck?" I was literally on my way down to talk to my assistant Glenn Stewart when Stephane Dacosta said to me, "Hey, Coach, what do you think of going to the other forecheck?" It's great that he felt comfortable enough—and he wasn't questioning what we were doing, it was more about the fact that he's a pretty good hockey mind too. He believed that I would listen and make a viable decision, and we did—I made a change right then and there. What effect did it have? Who knows? I'm not saying that changed the game, but I think that people have more of a tendency to believe in things that they come up with to a certain extent, so all of a sudden, not that they didn't buy into how we were forechecking, but now they're fully invested. They're fully invested in what we were doing. Again, what effect it had, who knows? But they believed that this change would have a positive effect, and the result at the end of the game was a good one. So whether it really changed the result or not, it's unclear, but it strengthened their belief in what we were doing.

JL: The 2010–11 season was one of great success at Merrimack, unparalleled success—

the Hockey East Championship game, the NCAA tournament—how much did that season's success convince your players of the trueness of your vision?

MD: You know what, I think it happened before. The outcomes or results are the benefit of the process. Do you win because you believe, or do you believe because you win? If you're waiting to win before you believe in what you're doing, you're not going to win. So whether it's belief in how we play, belief in yourself, belief in your teammates, whatever it is, there needs to be some semblance of belief before you have success. The results? That's all they are results, and you can't control those. But what you can control are the building blocks, the process that leads up to that, so that's really what we talk about the most and kind of let the results speak for themselves. So I think there was a belief system or process in place before 2010, or maybe it happened during it, who knows? It's really tough to believe when things aren't going your way. You can go back to the Bible there, with Job. It's easy to believe when things are going well. Ironically, you really need to believe when things aren't going well, and that's also the hardest time to do it, so I tip my cap to the Chris Bartons of the world, the Adam Rosses of the world, Karl Stollery, Joe Cannata, guys that believed in what we were doing before the results were there. It's easy to believe when all of a sudden you start having success.

JL: What tangible types of plays best illustrate your definition of how best to carry out your belief systems and mission of how to play winning hockey at Merrimack College (i.e., blocking shots, winning battles, etc.)?

MD: We talk about playing a team game and we talk about being selfless, and I think sometime the biggest indicator of a belief system is the guys that aren't playing. There are always a number of guys whose number don't get called, and if you've got a good belief system in place, they're not rooting against their teammates, and they're not hoping that the team fails so they can get in. They believe that if they work harder, they're going to have a chance to get into that lineup. And it's about their teammates in the sense that we're going to cheer for them, but it's not us against them. It's not me against the next left winger in the lineup, or me against the power play defenseman whose ice time I want. You're working toward that, but it's about a team, so we've had guys who are healthy scratches who were just as excited for wins as the guys who were playing. And they were not happy about not playing, but they didn't let it show and they didn't let it affect how they approach their training. Look at Simon Demers, I think that's a perfect example. His career was not as stellar as Karl Stollery's, and then there's Simon at the end of his career playing, getting quality minutes because he stuck with it and because he believed in what we were doing, and he didn't let lack of success or lack of playing time affect his approach. It's great because trust me when I tell you, there was no one on our team that was happier for them then Simon.

JL: A belief or vision needs to be unwavering. What is your message to the team if doubt should creep in?

MD: One of my favorite stories from Eric Capetula, and it's not only a favorite, but it's very tragic, but Eric Capetula in the program is watching a video of an actual battle with his platoon leader. It was just the two of them and whoever was running the training protocol. And it shows two American soldiers who are basically hemmed in by the enemy. And the enemy is getting closer and closer, and the Americans continue to fight, and at one point it is so close and so imminent that one soldier tapped the other soldier on the shoulder, and they shook hands. And his platoon leader looked at him and said, "That will not be us." And I think Eric took that as, "We won't put ourselves in that situation." And his commander said, "No, that will not be us. If you tap me on the shoulder, I'm going to shoot you." The gist of it is, you can't let that doubt creep in. You need to be mentally strong enough. Everybody's been on a team where you're trailing in a game, and someone feels the need to say, "Hey, we're not going to lose this." You shouldn't even be thinking that. But it's difficult to do. It is. It's very difficult to do. But the best teams I've been a part of, whether they're up a goal, down a goal, or tied, it doesn't matter what the situation is, it doesn't matter the time, they believe they're going to pull it out. Just look at BU in 2009 when they're down two goals to Miami with under two minutes to play, and I remember a team at Princeton, the championship team at Princeton, was down 4-1 going into the third against Cornell. I was part of a team at Boston College that was trailing UNH by a similar score in a Hockey East semifinal. People ask me all the time, how are you going to do it tonight? I kind of laugh and think to myself, "I'll let you know after the second period," because the teams I've been a part of that have been the best. There's just a feeling that exists, and it's tough to put a word in it—maybe belief is it—but when they're going into the third period, regardless of the score or the situation, they're going to win. And so having that mindset where that will never be us, I think it's really important, and it's also very difficult to cultivate.

JL: Getting back to flexibility for a moment. When installing your belief system here at Merrimack, how much do you rely on communicating your vision to your assistant coaches and have they given you suggestions on how to achieve results from their perspective?

MD: Yes, it is a completely interactive process. If there is a weakness in how we approach things, and I'm sure there is, I may involve everyone too much. I love to hammer things out behind closed doors. I'm not someone who just comes in with a mandate and says, "This is what we're doing" and "I know everything, and this is the blueprint." I've got some good ideas that I've taken from other people and added my own wrinkles into, but I brought these assistant coaches in to coach and bring out the best in me, so, no, there's always inclusion. It's an inter-active process, and then once the standards are set, our job in terms of the coaching or the leading of young men is set a stan-dard, communicate that standard, com-municate that standard as best you can, so that everyone understands it, and then you need to hold everyone in the organization accountable for the standards. And I think that when you really have it going, then the next step occurs. And if you're confident enough to empower your own players, then they need to hold each other accountable. And that's something we were able to do in 2010–11 that we didn't do as good of a job at in 2011–12, so the buck stops with me, but setting a standard and communicating that are two of the first steps toward putting in a culture you can believe in.

JL: Who was your most important influence in college hockey in terms of shaping your beliefs and why?

MD: I can think of two people, John Cunniff, the late John Cunniff, who played at Boston College, a South Boston native, who played for the Hartford Whalers, coached the Bruins, and ended his career with the New Jersey Devils. On a number of fronts, he is someone who had an unbelievable effect on my passion for the game. My dad used to print his summer school hockey school brochures, so I used to get to go for free, and I'd go as many weeks in the summer as my parents would take me there. He has such a passion for the game, and he was so far ahead of the rest of the United States in terms of taking advantage of some of the Russian training protocols. Off ice, on ice, he just had such a passion for the game that it resounded with me, and it really cemented my love of the game. And then Don Cahoon, who I worked with twice, once at Princeton, and then another time at UMass. Again, his passion for the game and his sincerity, the confidence he had to openly admit failure, yet also confident enough to spread the success around. And his ability to rally a group—I often kid around and say if there was one game to win and I couldn't coach it, he's the guy. I've seen him turn ships around that I thought were sinking. So it's those two guys for sure. There have been a lot of people, though, that I've learned from. I learn every day, whether it's Darren Yopyk, Glenn Stewart, or Curtis Carr. If I've done anything right, it's surround myself with good people.

JL: If you could identify one player from the 2011–12 team that best exemplified the personification of Merrimack hockey that best illustrated your belief systems, who would it be and why?

MD: It's really hard because I don't like to single people out. But I'll say, there was a guy, ironically of very few words, Karl Stollery, who definitely met our standard. He came in from a championship RBC team in Camrose and understood what it took and was willing to elevate his game while he was here. And again, there are a number of guys that I could mention, but the reason I bring him up is he is a man of few words, but what he said up at Maine at the end of our season this year, to me, I'm going to make sure that's up on one of our walls. And it's very simple—when you put this jersey on, put it on with pride. And that wasn't the case when we first got here as a staff. And because of the efforts of guys like Karl and Joe Cannata, Adam Ross, Chris Barton, Fraser Allan, J. C. Robitaille, Pat Bowen, Brandon Sadlowski, you can just go right on down the list of guys that helped change this program. Now those words have way more meaning than they ever have.

JL: In summation, what are your thoughts regarding how anyone can harness the power of belief?

MD: Well, it can't be empty. I go back to the idea that you have to focus on the tangible, because it's a very abstract concept, the concept of belief. What do you believe in? Personally, I believe that if you work hard enough and long enough, good things will happen. I remember saying this our second year when our team scored thirty-seven goals in thirty-four games—I cannot tell you when good things are going to happen, but it's been my experience in life that if you work hard enough long enough, good things will happen. And I can only hope that the guys on that team took as much pride in the recent successes that we've had as the guys that were here, because they didn't reap those rewards, yet they sowed a lot of those seeds. Guys like Rob Ricci, who is actually coming back here to train this summer, sacrificed a ton to change the culture of the program. And hopefully he's as proud of it as the guys that took part in it.

Closing Thoughts on Belief

Belief is, to me, something that can be thought of as a feeling of certainty that you can accomplish what you set out to achieve. To a large extent, the learning opportunities you experience in life create a set of tangible pool of evidence that will help support these feelings of certainty. And a related aspect of belief is faith—faith in your abilities, faith in your colleagues, or your teammates, whatever your support system may be. This faith, or trust, is developed over time. A common synonym for belief is confidence, which we will discuss at length with Boston College's Jerry York in chapter 10. But in its most basic form, belief is the feeling inside of an individual striving for excellence who knows that he or she has what it takes to get the job done. And, as Coach Dennehy eloquently mentioned, one must strive to be mentally tough and not allow the power of negative thinking to incapacitate your belief system. Easier said than done, but if we are willing to persevere and have unshakable faith and belief, we can move mountains in any area of our lives.

Belief needs to be unwavering, and that is difficult when your faith and belief is something not popular among the outside world but is relevant to you. When you know something is right and worth fighting for, but others don't see it and attempt to influence and criticize you, that is where you need the power of conviction the most. I remember a song that was popular back in the 1980s, recorded by Tracey Ullman called "They Don't Know." In the song, she is expressing her feelings for someone but the whole world is against her choice. She indicates that her eyes are wide open and "they don't know about us." Throughout the whole story, she stands true to her beliefs, convictions, and feelings despite the overwhelming negative opinion. The person in the video of the song that represents her interest? It was none other than Paul McCartney of the Beatles.

Sports in general is rife with examples of belief in action, more specifically having faith in your teammates to carry out your mission and your objectives. Perhaps no bigger example is in the game of football, in which the quarterback has faith that his offensive line will protect him and watch his back. Also as a quarterback, having faith that your receivers will run the correct routes and be in a position to make plays. In college hockey, a coach can diagram a play during a timeout and expect execution of that play. The players may not understand the logic or the wisdom of the call (hopefully they do!), but they don't question it because they have faith in their coach and belief that the play will work. On a larger and much more important scale, the military is another example of faith and belief in action. When the commanding officer executes the order, it is followed without question, because of the faith and belief that those higher up have the appropriate reasons for designing the battle plan.

In conclusion, when you approach in your life any endeavor, have faith in your abilities and trust people that you come to count on. Believe in your heart that you have what it takes to get the job done. Mark Dennehy believed in his vision of creating success at Merrimack College, and there is nothing you can't do if you believe in your heart that it is done.

Preparation

Tim Whitehead, University of Maine

Tim Whitehead completed twelve years of service in the hockey program at the University of Maine, culminating in the 2012–2013 campaign. Under Coach Whitehead's tutelage, Maine has made seven NCAA tournament appearances and two national championship game appearances. Tim compiled a record of 250-171-54 in his career at Maine. He succeeded Coach Shawn Walsh as an assistant in 2001–2002, following Coach Walsh's passing, and led the Black Bears to the NCAA title game in St. Paul, Minnesota, losing to Minnesota in overtime after being named interim head coach. Coach Whitehead was honored with the Spencer Penrose Coach of the Year award in 2002 for his coaching excellence. He became just the third coach in school history on April 8, 2002. He also has had coaching experience at UMass Lowell, with five years as a head coach and five more as an assistant as well as coaching at Middlebury College for two seasons.

We now turn to the subject of preparation. Preparation is the vital element of success necessary to do your best. When it comes time to execute your game plan in life, you will perform to the best of your ability if you have rehearsed the possible outcomes ahead of time. To address this all-important topic, I travelled up to beautiful

Orono, Maine, to discuss this subject with Maine head hockey coach Tim Whitehead. Hockey is no different than any other endeavor—prep work is as critical here as is every other endeavor in life. So let's hear what Coach Whitehead has to say on this topic, and I'll give you my thoughts at the end of the chapter.

JL: How crucial do you feel preparation is related to success and how do you go about ensuring perfect preparation for Maine hockey as games approach?

TW: Well, I do certainly feel that preparation is one of the keys to success, and like everything in life, we are what we repeatedly do, so if we prepare properly, we increase the odds of success when it's time to perform. And certainly from my aspect here with Maine hockey, we put a lot of emphasis on proper preparation, and so that means every single day doing things the right way. And if you do that consistently day after day, week after week, year after year, then you have a strong program.

JL: To what extent does attention to detail play in proper preparation?

TW: Certainly, attention to detail is always important in any area of life that you want to excel in, and certainly, in hockey, attention to detail is crucial. It covers everything from how you warm up, to how you practice, to how you warm down, how you compete, and how you carry yourself off the ice. Without a doubt, attention to details is absolutely essential. Executing details properly is absolutely essential to setting a foundation for success.

JL: Is it possible to discern from practices whether or not your team is properly prepared or does that manifest itself more in game type situations?

TW: Well, usually when you watch a team practice consistently over a period of time, you can certainly get a pretty good idea if that team is prepared or not, but sometimes, usually you can see it even just by watching the team play. You can see the execution of detail, the focus of the players, their conditioning, and areas like that, but that's not always the case. That's why we play the games—you never know what's going to happen. There are, obviously, other elements that are out of your control, but I think that is the key to preparation—to focus on what you can control and practicing things the right way and repetition of the right skills, so that when you get in the game there is less room for error. There's less chance that bad luck will have a factor in the game. Obviously there could be good luck too. I think the key as far as details is just executing things on a consistent basis. If you do that, then nine times out of ten good things will happen.

JL: Are there any types of things that might indicate to you and your coaching staff that your team might not be as properly prepared for whatever reason as you would like during a game as it unfolds? And if so, how do you and the coaching staff get that back on track?

TW: Well, it is difficult to get it back on track if you haven't prepared properly and that's why it is so important to prepare. It's just like taking an exam in school. If you haven't prepared properly throughout the semester, you can cram and do reasonably well, but to do well on a consistent basis in the classroom, you've got to prepare consistently well. And hockey is the same—if you're cramming at the last minute for a game or relying on in-game adjustments to dictate the outcome of a game, there's less chance you're going to win over the long haul. It may work on certain nights, and obviously there are things we can do if we find within a game that we're not prepared in a certain area. Of course we can make some adjustments, but you are rolling the dice then. So the key is to try and anticipate the scenarios that are going to happen in the game, so that there are less times that you have to ad-lib and fly from the seat of your pants. So that's what preparation is all about—practicing all the different scenarios that might come about and might occur, so when different things happen in the game, as they always do, you're prepared for it.

JL: Isn't it true that preparation is defined not only by physical preparation but also by mental preparation as well? And is the mental impact more important in your view?

TW: Yes, and who knows what the percentages of the importance of mental versus physical are, but one thing is for sure, you can't just rely on one. You have to be mentally and physically prepared, and you have to be mentally and physically tough to succeed at the highest level. From a mental perspective, a lot of that comes from paying the price physically, building self-confidence, and building confidence in each other by paying the price from a physical standpoint. Developing your physical and mental toughness is certainly a crucial aspect to performing well and being mentally strong in games, there's no doubt about that. And they are tied together, they certainly are in any elite sporting event. If you're not physically and mentally prepared for that event, you're going to be in trouble.

JL: It has been said also in the course of preparation, visualizing the success you want to achieve is a critical skill. Is that something that any or all your players engage in, and how much value do you place on that as a technique?

TW: Certainly, preparation visually can be very helpful. You see a lot of Olympic athletes doing that, depending on the sport more or less of that is done, but in hockey you see it all the time. Players prior to games with their eyes closed visualizing certain situations. Goaltenders are probably the biggest users of visualizations for obvious reasons— their job is very contained. They can visualize those situations, and I think it's effective for all players. Certainly we encourage our players to visualize the types of situations they might be in—whether it's with the puck, without the puck, situations where they're in confrontations after the whistle—all kinds of different areas where you can visualize yourself making the right choices. And if you do that in advance, you've got a much better chance of actually making the right choice when the pressure is on.

JL: Well, it's almost as if you can use a baseball analogy—when you're in the field playing defense, you always anticipate, "What am I going to do if this ball gets hit to me?" Really, you can draw the same parallels in hockey, can't you? Such as, "What am I going to do if the puck comes to me?" or "Where do I need to be?" that sort of thing?

TW: Without a doubt. And as you probably know from those that specialize in visualization, the more colorful you can make that picture in your head, the more senses you can get involved in—where there's the smell of the rink, the color of the uniforms, or the temperature in the arena, the wind in your face—all those kinds of things that will all contribute to the strength of the visual picture that comes to you. So if you are going to visualize, you want to make it as detailed and as bright as you can so that it sticks.

JL: Describe the relationship between preparation and confidence. Would it be fair to say that the more prepared your hockey team is, the more confident your hockey team will be in executing their game plan?

TW: You've hit it right on the head, without a doubt. If you want confidence, you can't just say, "I know I can win." Everyone wants to win. I think one of my favorite quotes is "It's not the will to win that separates people, it's the will to prepare to win." That's what separates the elite from the average. And we've all heard that, but it's really true. I think without a doubt the will to prepare is what separates the elite athletes, and so I think it's just a focus that we have with our team every day, and it's no different from the analogy I mentioned in the classroom—if you're not studying each day, it becomes very difficult to ratchet it up in a twenty-four-hour period cramming for an exam. It might work once in a while—you might hit the right buttons on a certain test or essay—but in the long run, you're not going to get strong results. And the same is true in sports.

JL: Take us through a typical week of preparation for Maine hockey after a Saturday night game as you get ready for your next opponent on the following Friday night. What would a general week of preparation be like?

TW: For us, it starts immediately after the game, getting closure on the Saturday night game, taking some time to rest, and put it behind us one way or the other. You shower it off and you move on to the next week, the next challenge. So Monday, we review video and make sure that we do get full closure on that weekend and learn what we can from it, both positive and negative, whether it's a win, a loss, or a draw. So win lose or draw, we want to make sure that we've gotten better as a result of that competition. Then our typical week is weight training, video, practice on the ice, in the classroom, and in the community. And from a social aspect, making sure we make the right decisions. And then once again, we revisit video on our upcoming opponent so that we prepare as best we can. But the confidence, as you mentioned before, comes from the daily preparation in every aspect. And that's when we're self-confident going into the Friday night game—is when we've prepared all week. Relying on a Knute Rockne speech right before the game or in between periods, you need that once in a while without a doubt, and you can obviously use every tool at your disposal, but if you're relying on that game in and game out, then there is something missing in your preparation.

JL: In terms of offseason preparation for the coming season, what does that entail for Maine hockey players? Is it strictly physical conditioning, or are there other elements involved?

TW: Well, again, it comes back to daily habits. A lot of it is physical—preparing the right way with your weight training, your conditioning, your speed work, whatever your points of emphasis are that you want to improve. Obviously, the entire team has a workout that they're doing on their own over the summer, but with individual points of emphasis of course. Each player is unique, and it should be viewed that way, and has areas of strengths and areas of weakness, so it needs to be very player specific. But I think again it's not only the physical workout, and one guy could get a lot better and the other guy could just remain the same because he may not be preparing in other ways. He may not be eating the right things or taking care of himself socially, maybe not getting the right amount of sleep. There are so many aspects to your preparation that come into play over the summer, and certainly your personal daily habits are at the top of the list.

JL: In a nutshell, moving away from hockey for a moment, what general strategies can you recommend to people who want to master the concept of preparation in all areas of their life?

TW: I would encourage them to focus on executing things daily, doing things the right way, day in and day out. And if they do that consistently, whatever their passion may be, if they're focused on it day in and day out and executing it in the right way on a daily basis, they are going to dramatically increase the odds of success. And they are going to increase their self-confidence, and in their ability to actually perform in the key moments, whatever their line of work may be. So again I think it does come back to preparing on a daily basis—that's what is going to give you the confidence to really reach great heights in whatever your passion is.

Closing Thoughts on Preparation

Preparation. It is the foundational key to success. To be more precise, it is systematic detailed preparation that ensures successful results. I like to think of preparation in those terms. Let's look at each part of that in turn. Systematic—meaning that there cannot be a haphazard approach to preparation. You need to know exactly what is ahead of you and what you need to execute in precise terms. And detailed—meaning, every little thing is accounted for—all your i's are dotted, and your t's are crossed. As Coach Whitehead said, the more prepared you are for a situation, the more likely you will succeed because you have already played the scene in your mind and your subconscious mind will then unlock the vital forces within you to execute your game plan.

To illustrate the concept of preparation further, I like to refer to my broadcasting preparation I used to get ready to broadcast a Merrimack game. Before I bought the software I currently use on my computer, I composed what are termed spotting boards—visual tools that we broadcasters use to quickly identify key facts and data about the game we are going to cover. I would buy an eighteen-by-twenty-two-size poster board at Staples and would completely cover every inch of that board with colored markers on every key piece of information that I would need for the game. Mind you, I would never be able to use every bit of that info—much of it will be unused—but the point is you have to be ready and capture all the information you can because you never want to miss anything relevant. For a Friday night game, I would work on our team, Merrimack, on Tuesday. It would take me eight hours of work to complete the board. That's a full day. On Wednesday, I would work on our opponent and repeat the process. Eight hours of prep for them too. If we had a weekend where we had a second opponent on Saturday, I would work on them on Thursday with an eight-hour board. Friday morning would be reserved for another board to capture league standings, stats, and the like. By the time the work was done, I had a rainbow of colors splashed across the board with every tidbit of information I could accumulate. To learn more about my spotting board techniques, please visit my website at www.johnrleahy.com.

The result? When it was time to go on the air, I was confident. I knew that I was prepared, and nothing would get by me. As a broad-caster, there's nothing worse than something happening in a game, and you don't know about it because you have not prepared properly to do your job. My personal mission is to never let that happen.

Whatever your game plan is in life, take the time to prepare. Visualize what you need to accomplish, and make it a clear vision full of rich sensory detail, as Coach Whitehead alluded to. Replay the scene in your mind and then go to work to execute it. If you prepare well enough, you won't have to worry about performing when the time comes. You just will. Naturally.

CHAPTER 6

Accountability

Norm Bazin, University of Massachusetts at Lowell

Norm Bazin completed a historic two seasons behind the bench at UMass Lowell in 2011–2012 and 2012–2013 after a stellar playing career with the River Hawks. After the team finished 5-25-4 in 2010–2011, Coach Bazin stepped in and left his indelible mark of success on the club, guiding the River Hawks to an amazing 24-13-1 season, which included a mark of 17-9-1 in Hockey East. After missing the playoffs the season before, UMass Lowell made both the Hockey East tournament and the NCAA tournament, losing to Providence in the Hockey East tournament, and then defeating Miami in overtime before losing to Union in the East Regional Final of the NCAA tournament. In 2012–2013, he led the team to the Hockey East championship, the first ever in school history, followed by the first Frozen Four berth in school history. Coach Bazin was named Hockey East Coach of the Year for his efforts in both 2011–2012 and 2012–2013. He was also named a finalist for the Spencer Penrose Trophy as the National Coach of the Year in 2011–2012, then winning the award in 2012–2013. Norm coached two successful seasons at Hamilton College prior to returning to coach his alma mater, while also serving as an assistant at Colorado College, and at the University of Maine alongside Tim Whitehead. He compiled 32 goals and 36 assists in 134 career games with the River Hawks.

In this chapter, we will visit with UMass Lowell head coach Norm Bazin, as he speaks on the subject of accountability—taking personal responsibility and ownership for your successes and your failures. It is the "no excuses" mentality that we all need to embrace to ensure that we learn from our mistakes and prepare well for the future ahead. Coach Bazin's message truly resonated with his team in 2011–2012, and hopefully it will connect with you too. When Coach is finished with his thoughts, I'll give you my two cents.

> JL: Let's start with accountability as a means to success. How is this concept defined by you and how did it manifest itself in the UMass Lowell hockey season just past?

> NB: Well, it was an important part of our hockey club last year because coming into the season, there was certainly a period coming in where I didn't know any of these boys, and we needed to set a culture of accountability and how we wanted to approach each and every practice and games, so it was a big part of our season this past year.

> JL: You and I talked about the importance of establishing the concept of identity and how the River Hawks sought to establish their own identity last season—to what extent did personal accountability play in that process?

> NB: Well, it played a huge part. Our mission for the season was to reestablish our identity, but as part of that, having strong accountability in all facets of our program was a

mainstay. You know, I'm very simple in my rules and I'm very simple in my philosophy. The culture of accountability was a mainstay and a central theme.

JL: What steps must a college hockey player take in making accountability a priority?

NB: He needs to come to terms with where he's playing, who we are, and how we want to play the game. Our philosophy was simply we wanted to play fast, and we wanted to be an aggressive hockey club. Outside of the ice, we want every facet of our lives to be strong and to have strong accountability. And it starts in the classroom. Ninety percent of our hockey players will never get the opportunity to play in the NHL, and for those people, they'll need that degree for a long time. So we emphasize academics first and foremost, and we take the term "student athlete" very seriously. We have been the highest achieving male team on campus for the last five years, and we're proud of that. So it starts in the classroom. We have some very direct meetings with our hockey club at the start of the season on how they need to conduct themselves and how they want to be viewed, on campus, in the community, and on the ice. And they come up with the series of statements that we live by, and it goes back to accountability. So that goes back to showing up for class every single day, and doing the right thing so that they can actually maintain that high standard.

JL: Describe for us a scenario from last season that illustrated the process of accountability in action with the River Hawks.

NB: Well, there were several different instances where accountability was certainly illustrated by the team. We have a strong nucleus of leadership council, and they were able to emphasize accountability in many different ways. Each and every day, our habits dictate how we want to play the game. So for example, on the ice it would be playing with our sticks on the ice, stopping in front of the net, playing fast, which sounds like very simple things, but you constantly catch people not doing those things. So we then stop the practice and certainly emphasize how we want to play the game. Off the ice, it's showing up for class, which I mentioned earlier is a big part of things. And in the community, we have a standard we want to maintain with one hundred hours of community service, so these are all ways that we keep each other accountable. Being late for a meeting last year, that happened on a few occasions so those boys were forced to watch the game that night. So all those off-ice standards are put into play, and sometimes it is very difficult as a coach to emphasize that standard. But it is a standard that the kids came up with on their own, and that's why we hold true to it.

JL: You recently finished your first season here at UMass Lowell. When you first addressed the team upon taking over, what were your messages to the team about collective responsibility and accountability?

NB: My message was very simple. We were going to get back to playing strong, Lowell-type hockey. And that meant playing fast. That meant being aggressive. That meant being a very difficult team to play against. We did not focus on goals, but rather we focused on reestablishing our identity. And that was our mission for the season.

JL: A synonym for accountability might be thought of as humility. How closely from your perspective are those terms related?

NB: I think they are related closely. However, I feel the hockey culture in general, whether you're talking about Lowell or someone else, has a very humble background. Hockey is a great sport. And it's probably the humblest sport out there, especially at the pro level. But our guys have been very good people in the community, in the classroom, and on the ice. And when you talk about humility, it's very important to have that humility as a strong characteristic in your dressing room because that's how you give back to the community and they support you in return.

JL: We've talked about the importance of taking personal responsibility in terms of how a college hockey player might approach the game of ice hockey, but how does this concept translate into other areas of life?

NB: Accountability touches each and every part of your life. Whether you're talking about the classroom or you're talking about the community, I think once you determine as a young man that you'll get much more out of what you have once you start giving back, then it's a tremendous experience for you in college. And it's such a great four years of their life. They quickly find out that accountability is everything. Our boys had quite an opportunity to get to know a lot of good people within our community because they give back to it first. And because of that, they're receiving the support that they would like for the hockey club, so in my opinion, it goes very far and it's in every aspect of their lives.

JL: How much of an impact did your captains have on spreading the importance of accountability, and how was that received by the rest of the team?

NB: Our leadership core and captains serve a very important role in setting and maintaining accountability with our hockey club. We were very fortunate this season to have a solid captain who led by example and represented our team well on and off the ice. However, our coaching staff was equally impressed with our leadership core. We would meet with them on Mondays to discuss the team climate and map out the upcoming week. That group was instrumental in giving me a pulse of where our team was mentally and physically. They then were responsible for helping to communicate our expectations for helping to communicate our expectations to the rest of the club for that week.

JL: As you reflect back on the season that just ended, what lessons were learned about the importance of accountability and collective personal responsibility?

NB: We received a great deal of lessons. The hockey season, as you know, is the longest sports season of any other college sport. It's chock-full of adversity. I think when you have a group of young men that come together and truly take ownership of their hockey club, then they feel a greater sense of responsibility for each other, and in turn, for themselves in how they act and how they perform. So I think our guys throughout the season learn many great lessons that they'll take with them for a long, long time in every aspect of their lives.

JL: In summation, what do you advise as a strategy or strategies to those interested in cultivating the concept of accountability in any area of life?

NB: Determine what your philosophy is, first and foremost, whether it's in the business world, or whether it's in education or on a sports team. It's important to determine what your philosophy is and what your mission is going to be. And then having a high standard in maintaining that trek and that

course. If you do that, and then have ram-
ifications for those that don't stay on task,
then you can go a long way with the group
that you have.

Closing Thoughts on Accountability

Accountability is collective responsibility. It's everyone that makes up the fabric of a team doing what needs to be done and not making excuses when things go wrong. The great author Dale Carnegie once said in his best-selling book, *How To Win Friends and Influence People*, "When you are wrong, admit it quickly and emphat-ically." Likewise, if you are on a team at work, whether it's in business or on the hockey rink, take responsibility for your effort and perfor-mance and adjust things when necessary. Coach Bazin illustrated this when talking about the players who were late for a meeting—there was a consequence involved. They didn't play in the game that night. When not meeting a standard in place, it illustrates the importance of responsibility and teaches accountability.

My favorite story about accountability that I like to relate to is taken from my time in mental health. For fifteen years, I worked with the mentally retarded and developmentally delayed popula-tions, of various degrees of impairment. I would observe people with behavioral and cognitive problems struggling with managing their lives. Many of my clients were lower-functioning individuals who could not process and reason sufficiently, but I also worked with higher-level men and women who were in fact able to understand reasoning and logic. It is with the latter of these folks that I will relate my story.

Just prior to an individual acting out in a behavioral way that would cause harm to himself or herself or others, I would say some-thing like, "Okay, now think about what you are going to do here before you act. If you do this behavior, then you're going to lose your privileges. Is this what you want? On the other hand, if you pull yourself together and calm down so we can talk about it, then you'll get a reward." (Whatever that reward might be, relative to the client.)

In other words, what I was trying to do is help the person to take accountability. I was trying to let him or her know that if x happens, then y will occur as a result. This is the key to behavior modification. To borrow a term from college hockey, I wanted to create a culture in the client's mind that he or she is responsible for what happens to him or her as a direct result of their behavior—they are responsible or accountable for what happens to them. If they lost a privilege, it was because they acted out. Once you establish that connection, you have the key to making people personally responsible. And if you can build in natural consequences for behavior, that has been shown to be the most effective method to shape behavior. In college hockey, if a player violates a code of conduct, he or she will sit and not play. The loss of ice time is a natural consequence for the misdeed, and the player learns that their behavior is the reason for the end result, which helps them be accountable.

There are no shortcuts to success. Everyone needs to be held to a higher standard. That's the essence of accountability. And once everyone is fully invested in what the goals of the team are, they are more likely to be involved and take ownership when things go wrong.

Consistency

Don Cahoon, University of Massachusetts

Coach Don (Toot) Cahoon finished his twelfth season behind the UMass bench in 2011–12 and his twenty-fifth as a college hockey coach. Under Coach Cahoon's leadership, the Minutemen enjoyed their best play in school history, particularly the 2006–2007 season, which saw UMass earn their first NCAA playoff berth and first NCAA win, a 1-0 victory over Clarkson in OT. Coach Cahoon also led the Minutemen to a fifth ranked national ranking in 2007–2008, their highest ranking of all time. Coach Cahoon has also coached 2011–2012 NHL MVP and Stanley Cup winner Jonathan Quick of the Los Angeles Kings. Prior to his time at Massachusetts, he was the head coach at Princeton from 1991–98, where he rebuilt the hockey program there, and also, he served as an assistant to Jack Parker at Boston University, his alma mater. He also began his coaching career at Lehigh in the 1973–74 season, while also serving as head coach at Norwich University.

The next chapter deals with the concept of consistency. The pursuit of excellence is what we all chase. But what good is the process if you only strive to be good once in a while? Would it not be of value to align your pursuit of excellence in such a way that you develop consistent habits that allow you to always be at the top of your game?

Let's visit this topic with the former head coach of the University of Massachusetts, Don (Toot) Cahoon, and get his thoughts on this crucial topic. As always, check in at the end of this chapter and I'll wrap up the chapter with my thoughts.

> JL: Vince Lombardi once said that you don't do things right once in a while, you do them right all the time. Let's talk about this principle of consistency from the standpoint of UMass hockey. How do you and your staff approach the important topic of practicing and subsequently playing consistently well with your players?

> DC: Well, the first thing we do is establish a code of conduct, and you have to establish what the expectation is on that front. So it's how they behave in the locker room, but it goes even farther as to how they behave on campus, how they behave in their dormitories, the way they present themselves to the community—that sets the tone for who we are. And then now, what the expectation is on our athletic front is based on a discipline, a mandate from the coaches in that this is an always type of thing, versus "Hey, sometimes we'll do it this way or sometimes we'll do it that way." And that's quite honestly, given my personality, that's been a major shift in my thinking probably over the last thirty years. You know, I used to give more gray area, some more room. Now, I think it's more black and white with what we do and how we do it.

JL: Do you agree that being consistent is defined by the habits you engage in, and if you see a player who is exhibiting bad habits, how do you approach changing them?

DC: I think you offer them some advice. You create some protocol for him to follow, and you try to get him to develop that protocol a little bit on his own, but at the same time with some help, or some mentoring, if you will. After a certain period in time, as much as we recruit you and tell you we'll do whatever we can do for you, at the end of the day you're here to make us happy. I'm not here to make you happy. When we've got the method, we expect you to follow the methodology.

JL: In terms of reinforcing consistency among your players, many coaches reward players who demonstrate consistent play with more playing time. Is that a philosophy you sub-scribe to, and are there other tangible things you can do to reinforce consistency?

DC: I think we all like to know what we are get-ting. So, for example, Brett Watson was our captain a couple of years ago here. He was not a big-time goal scorer, but he was abso-lutely our best defensive forward, and he was a great face-off guy and penalty killer. And I knew what I was going to get from him every single day. And his life is built that way—he was a 3.8, 3.9 student, an honors student in the Eisenberg school, a big-time kid in terms of personality and leadership.

And so that kid gets a lot of playing time with me. He probably got as much playing time as James Marcou, who was a big-time offensive player. So, yes, I value that a great deal.

JL: There is a player you had here by the name of Jonathan Quick of the Los Angeles Kings, who had tremendous success this season, a Stanley Cup winner in fact, and the foundation of his success has been his consistent solid play. You saw firsthand him develop as a goaltender here. Talk about his ascension into the NHL and describe how he developed his consistent skill over time.

DC: Well, I think Jon was truly a superior athlete, and he had a physical makeup that gave him a distinct advantage over the people he was playing against all along. So I would never suggest that he came here raw, completely raw, and then all of a sudden became the great talent that he has become. I think he had some real good coaching at Avon Old Farms; they did a wonderful job with him. But I think most of it stems from his approach mentality and his emotional growth. He had these physical tools— Jimmy Stewart was the goaltender here, he had worked in professional hockey, and he had Darren Puppa at RPI, who won a national championship, and we also had Gabe Winer here who was a credible goalie in his own right. Not the athlete that Jon is, but a credible goaltender at this level who won big games. He got to be challenged by

Gabe, split duties in his first year as opposed to having this whole thing handed to him and had to battle through that whole process to make that ascension toward being the number 1 guy. And I think that truly helped him. He also stumbled along the way. A lot of people learn from their mistakes—the smart ones do, anyways—and Jon had some stumbles along the way that he dealt with, and he dealt with them on a mature level. He got some help in the process, and he grew emotionally. And I believe that once he got to LA, having dealt with the Manchester Monarchs and some of the trials and tribulations of that situation, getting to LA with Billy Ranford and Dean Lombardi, as well as all of the other people who were involved with him on a regular basis, gave him some ultimatums and gave him some directions. And he took full advantage of it and became that consistent athletic performer that he was capable of being, but he had to make that growth before he could realize the great success that he's having right now.

JL: Talk about the relationship between consistency and decision making when it comes to making plays on the ice. It seems simple, but making more quality decisions on the ice will lead to more consistent play. Is it really that simple?

DC: Well, I think the simpler, the happier quite honestly. I think guys sometimes try to do too much too often, and if you look at the highest level of play, like the Stanley Cup Playoffs, the recent playoffs, the Olympic games, or any big-time competition, you always hear the coaches tell the players to stay within themselves, make the play that's there, and don't try to create too much because that will get you in trouble. And I think that's a consistent mindset of understanding what you can do in a certain situation. Make the simple play and a lot of good plays together, as I like to tell the guys, a lot of singles lead to a lot of runs being scored. If you try to hit it out of the park every time, the percentages are really working against you.

JL: How big a role does your captains and upperclassmen play in establishing consistent habits on the team, especially with regards to the incoming freshmen?

DC: Well, I think that's a year-to-year process. We work with the leadership of our team, and we try to establish it and try to get them to understand what role they need to play. And then you've got so many different personalities that end up in a position of leadership, and they need to learn how to manage that a little bit. And some years are better than others. Some years you really have to rely on some of the younger guys that maybe have better qualities along those lines to be able to take the lead and be able to at least guide the team. And yet you have to be careful of ignoring the older guys in the program that have established themselves and who have put a lot of work into the program. So you can't ignore them, so you have to learn to manage that and balance that. And any team of any merit that I've been a part of has had a leadership quotient that's been pretty high. And the teams that lack it usually have a problem trying to get the big job done at the end.

JL: Video analysis is becoming more and more common when breaking down tendencies for teaching purposes. For those that might be unfamiliar with the role that it plays, what types of things could that show you as a coaching staff with regards to developing and installing more consistent habits?

DC: Well, there are many tools that we have at our disposal. From a coaching standpoint, it helps us make an analysis of what's happened in the course of the game or sometimes in the course of a week, because we'll often run videos on practice times and in practice situations. So we'll get to look before we assemble for practice situations as to what has taken shape, and maybe devise a practice that's relative to what we've watched on tape. Then it goes to the individual player where we can give him segments of his game that we think need work, and we can break it down to its simplest form. It might be a simple forechecking exercise, it might be a power play situation, or it might be a penalty kill. It could also be giving the goaltenders different scoring opportunities where we'd like to consider them playing things differently, or we want to make them mindful of a certain technique that they're being taught that they might be resisting a little bit, so it's invaluable. In between periods, I might want to look at the way that the other team is forechecking us, and I'll ask my director of hockey ops to give me all the forechecks that period that Merrimack put on us, and so maybe then I'll look at about ten forechecks in the course of that period that took shape. And then I'll try to come up with an exit strategy or come up with some type of conversation with my team. So it has great application to what we do, and I think this has taken shape in all sports right now, and certainly in the team sports.

JL: We have been taking a great deal about the on-ice habits of players, but probably the most important aspect of consistency with young men of this age is their approach to good habits and choices outside of the rink, such as their studies, social decision-making skills, things of that nature. What is your personal philosophy that you convey to your team when addressing this topic?

DC: Well, as much as we want them to integrate themselves into the community and into the student body, we let these guys know that that they are different than the rest of the student body. They can't be living their lives as if they're just an incoming freshman that's just joining the other students, and they're going to be able to engage themselves in all

of the activities that the general student pop-
ulation can. They've made sacrifices their
entire life to bring their skill set to the level
it is right now. To be given this opportunity,
this privilege we'd like to refer to it as, to be a
part of this program, to be a part of Hockey
East, and to be a part of Division 1 NCAA
hockey, we start by making sure they understand that. And then obviously the men-
torship of the upperclassmen plays a large
role in making sure that the younger players
understand what is acceptable and what is
unacceptable behavior. And we have a lot of
eyes and ears around campus, and I make
sure that it's very clear to them—and I'll
even bring people in and introduce them to
the young student athletes—that people are
watching them. It's a privilege to be a part
of this program, and they are special names
and faces on campus, and they'll be treated
that way. But with that comes the responsibility to behave at a different level. So I love
the maturity of our guys, and at the same
time you look around this age group and
what goes on socially throughout colleges,
and you just hold your breath. You just cross
your fingers and hope that the right things
are taking shape with your group so that
it doesn't come back to bite you because it
could happen to any one of us.

JL: I talked with Providence coach Nate Leaman
and will be talking to Jerry York about this,
and it would be great to get your take, as it
is very appropriate to our discussion. Long
winning streaks are the ultimate tangible

measure of consistency. Boston College won nineteen games in a row last season as an example. When you have a streak of that magnitude, do you have to be more diligent to guard against falling into bad habits?

DC: I have to go back to the '70s, to the BU teams I was involved with—there was a twenty-two-game streak that I was a part of, but I haven't had the good fortune here at UMass to run off nineteen, or even at Princeton, where we had a couple of great teams, but we've had good runs. And a good run in my mind in this league is anytime you can run off six or seven in a row or more. And you know, I think kids are locked in, and this is the way that they want to identify themselves. They want to be student athletes, and they're so locked into what their responsibilities are on a daily basis, that's what makes it come together. And they're not keeping score. They're not playing the scoreboard; they're not putting wins up and saying, "Hey, that's seven in a row." What they're saying is we did a good job tonight, and what's next? And that's a really big part of it and having great character. And let's not underestimate the value of having great players.

JL: In summation, let's step away from the rink for a moment and discuss how anyone, regardless of their endeavors in life, can master this concept of consistency. What strategies do you feel would be most useful to achieve mastery in this area?

DC: I think you have to keep it a day-to-day process. You have to look at what you need to accomplish in a week and say, "Well, if I'm really consistent with my efforts in general, it will all shape out." I think you have to manage this on maybe even a two, three, or four-hour basis. So if I get up in the morning and I have x amount of work to do or something I need to accomplish, I know that I had better be locked in and take care of every detail and be consistent in my approach. Making sure that if I need so much rest, I get it. If I need so much fuel, I eat properly. And if I need help, I go find that help to assist me to achieve the goals that I am trying to attain. And I think the great salesmen of the world, the great managers of the world, the great coaches of the world, and the great players of the world all find a way to be more consistent on that front and be able to engross themselves in that type of lifestyle.

Closing Thoughts on Consistency

Consistency boils down to hard work, discipline, and persistence. The end result of consistency is the habits, or rituals, that we perform. And these habits can really become a self-fulfilling prophecy. Once good habits are formed, they become natural and second nature. Unfortunately, bad habits can also become a consistent pattern if we do not get the feedback we need to change them. As it relates to hard work, consistency can become close to perfection if you are diligent enough to work harder than anyone else. The great basketball star Larry Bird was once asked to do a McDonald's commercial in which he was required to miss a free throw. It took him upward of twelve attempts to miss one—he had conditioned himself for consistent success through his unrivaled work ethic. So it really comes down to doing the right things over and over until your habits are permanently installed.

Jack Edwards, the television voice of the Boston Bruins on NESN, is a perfect example of consistency in action. His preparation prior to a broadcast makes him consistently excellent game in and game out. Jack prepares better than anyone in the business. Every nugget on every player is accounted for. His preparation has become consistent habits, which ensure that he rarely if ever misses something in a broadcast. Jack even has salary data as part of his preparation, and he uses massive spreadsheets to code and analyze everything. The bottom line is that Jack is consistent in his approach—he prepares the same way over and over, to the point where his performance becomes excellent. And he takes no shortcuts.

Anyone who follows sports can argue that the New England Patriots have been the model franchise in terms of consistency. Bill Belichick's teams have been among the most consistently winning franchises in history. How do they do it? Committing to getting better every day, not allowing distractions, mastering techniques and fundamentals, and having respect for the opponent and the process, not to mention hard work. College hockey is no different—coaches like Jerry York and Jack Parker, to name just a few, win consistently because they understand all these elements, and they embrace these values, not just once in a while, but all the time.

CHAPTER 8

Focus

Jack Parker, Boston University

Jack Parker finished his career as one of the all-time leaders in head coaching victories. Retiring after the 2012–2013 season, Coach Parker amassed a total of 855 career wins, second all-time among active coaches and third all-time in winning percentage. He won more games at one single institution than any other coach in NCAA hockey history. He won three NCAA titles and coached BU to twenty-three NCAA tournament appearances, a record. Coach Parker also won the Spencer Penrose Memorial Trophy, the award for national coach of the year, three times. He has also been named New England Coach of the Year seven times, Hockey East Coach of the Year five times, is a member of the BU Hall of Fame, and has been the recipient of the NHL's Lester Patrick Award in 2010.

Focus. We talk about it and always strive to be focused on our goals. But focusing is easier said than done. There are so many distractions in our day-to-day world, and sometimes it feels like an impossible task to have the ability to truly be attentive to what's important. This chapter will talk about this key concept with Jack Parker, one of the most successful college hockey coaches of all time. Elite athletes need to develop the habit of laser-like focus and the ability to lock themselves in on their targets and goals. Listen to the words of Coach Parker as he gives us his thoughts on focus before my final summary at the end.

JL: The subject of focus, sometimes referred to as the subject of sustained attention. We see it in sports all the time. In college hockey at this level, there are so many potential distractions at any given point in time. As the season starts, how do you address your BU teams on how best to block out the negative and focus on the mission at hand?

JP: Well, one of the things we try to do is, we try to give them a short-term, midterm, and overall long view of what we'd like them to get accomplished for their season and how they can best go about it. We want them to be focusing on what's going on school-wise and what's going on training-wise in September. You can't win a big hockey game in September—you've got to get ready with off-ice stuff, and there's only a couple of days a week we're on the ice. So most of the time it's off-ice training, and it seems like it's a long way away to the hockey season. It's about doing the right thing today. And that means to get to class and get to study hall. Do the next right thing today—that means get to Mike Boyle and our weight training and conditioning situation and get that done. And the one day you're on the ice with us, do that well too. The idea is to juggle those things and don't come here thinking, "I'm going to have a good time because I'm a freshman in college, or I'm a sophomore in college." You'll automatically have a good time if you take care of business. You won't have any regrets that way either. The short-term focus is sometimes thought of like, "How important can Economics 101 be, I'm going to be a pro hockey player?" If you've got Economics 101 at ten in the morning, do a good job with that. If you've got practice in the afternoon, do a good job with that. If you've got a weight training and conditioning session after practice, then do a good job with that. Then, when you put your head on the pillow at the end of the day, then you've had a good day because you've done the right thing. And if you put a whole bunch of days like that together, then you'll have no regrets.

JL: Let's talk about your personal philosophy about focus. How do you define that?

JP: I think it's attention to detail and preparation to get ready for what's coming next, and it could be Tuesday where we're getting ready for a Friday night game, or it could be we're on the bench and my shift is coming up. It's different types of focus, but it always comes back to the same thing—you've got to find a way to have everything in perspective; to make sure you're thinking about what's important and first things first. So if it's Tuesday, it's about getting the game plan down or getting the drills down, doing a good job at practice. Or maybe it's a weight training day, and even though it won't have much effect on Friday's game it'll have an effect on the end of the season on how much bigger and how much stronger I can get, so it's almost like there are many different kinds of types of focuses on moments of your day or on future things that are coming down the road. It's like, "I've got to get a Christmas present, too, but it's only July." I don't have to get it yet.

JL: What in your opinion is the key to developing and subsequently maintaining laser-like focus as a consistent habit among college hockey players?

JP: I think it's a difficult thing because these kids have so many voices they're listening to—there's their hockey coach, then there's their family advisor, there's parents, then a lot of times these kids are drafted, so there's also the scout from the team that drafted them. So they have an awful lot of input, let's say, that sometimes it's not that important to them, or shouldn't be that important to them. So in the long run, they personally have to figure it out. They have to be able to do what's good for them to be ready for the next thing they're doing. And most of the focus we're concerned about is getting ready for the game. So for example, Friday preparation before practice—pre-game skates, pre-game meals, and all that stuff—the closer you get to game time, the more you should be getting yourself ready to go. And it's a very personal thing. Some kids like to sit at their locker and stare at the floor and go over things in their head. There's some kids that like to have music on and "veg out." some kids like to be the class clown because that takes the tension off. And I always tell my players that you're going to have to get ready for the game your own personal way. You've got to figure that out. We'll give you help about that, and we'll talk to you about it, but whatever you feel is best for you is what's best for you. But you can never let the way you prepare interfere with the way someone else is preparing. In reality, it's about getting ready for the game.

JL: Is it possible for a player to be over-focused or too amped up prior to a game, and if so, how do you manage that? And is that a bad thing?

JP: I think it's a very bad thing. People always ask me, "When do you start thinking about the Beanpot?" for example. We never talk about the Beanpot until the Saturday before, and once we play our Friday night game, then we'll talk about the Beanpot. Because kids can get too jacked up for it, too excited for it. The same thing holds true for the Hockey East tournament or the NCAA tournament. There's great movie called *The Hustler* in which Paul Newman plays a pool shark, and the guy that's handling him is talking to him, and he asks him how he feels, and he says, "I feel tight, but I feel good." And that's the only way I feel like I can describe it—you want to be on edge and ready to go, but not so much over that you're uptight. You want to feel good about it and feel comfortable about it, and the best way to do that—we keep telling our kids this—is if you've done the right things all week, then Friday and Saturday will take care of themselves. The preparation has a lot to do with it. Failing to prepare will be preparing to fail. And so, you can't just turn it on at seven on a Friday night. You've got to make the decision—you've got to do what's best for you in getting ready for it.

JL: To what extent do your BU players use visualization techniques to sharpen their focus and how valuable do you feel that technique is?

JP: I think visualization personally was great for me when I was playing, and I think it's a great tool. I think that there are some kids that don't like to think about it too. We prepare them in different ways. We give them three or four different ways to scout a team. There's some on-ice stuff that we walk through; there's some visual stuff that we show them on the video monitors and TVs; there's some handouts that we give; and there are also some chalk talks that we give. Some kids learn differently, some kids like it differently. Some kids use all three and they're comfortable. But I've coached guys that think that they're better off not knowing about the other team—and I don't think that's true—but they've gotten themselves into that. Again, the most important thing is how the player feels and is he ready?

JL: Coach, at times, off-ice distractions do occur. Last season your program dealt with a few of them. How did you ensure that your team retained its focus during those tough times, and how do you feel the team responded to your message?

JP: The message was pretty simple—that's happening to your teammates. That is not who we are, and in the end, I'm sure it will be shown that's not who they are either. In general, we had to get through this by focusing on what you're ready to do—focusing on what you can control and what you can't control. The difficult part about it was these are the best friends, very close guys, the guys that they have lunch with every day. This is the guy they sit down next to in the locker room, the guy they go to study hall with. And now they're not here anymore, it's as if somebody died in the dressing room, so that was difficult. And I thought the captains did a great job in refocusing. Of the first two guys we lost, we lost the first guy because we kicked him off the team, and the second guy we lost because he decided to leave and go play Major Junior A. That was in December, and our first game back after that was kind of a shock. Both were bad situations—one kid bailing out on his team and another kid getting in trouble. And both of those things were kind of a shock to the team. We went out and played Notre Dame right after Christmas, and we didn't play very well, and I was thinking, "Oh, boy, we lost our first two-line centers, and they think we're not going to be any good." And so we made a few changes as to who was going to take over those positions. It's amazing that when something bad happens to one person, then something good happens to somebody else. All of a sudden, some guys were playing on the power play, some guys were moving up on the lines to get more ice time, and everybody responded greatly I thought. People said to me, "We had a tough year last year," and I say, "Yeah, we had an awful year off of the ice, but we had a pretty good year on the ice." I was really pleased with the on-ice performance of our guys, and especially their focus in being able to maintain the idea that "I'm going to do the best I can in this situation," and we'll deal with the other situation later.

JL: Wayne Calloway once said that "Nothing focuses the mind better than the constant sight of a competitor who wants to wipe you off of the map." Do you feel that the ability to focus on being your best in a critical competitive situation is innate with athletes, or do you think it's more of a learned skill?

JP: I really think that it's a little bit of both. Some kids are born with poise. I remember talking to Chris Drury one time, and he had a penalty shot against BC in a big game, either the Beanpot or a playoff game. It might have even been a big game against BC in the regular season. He had a penalty shot and he scored. Everyone was happy, and we won that game. The next day, we were at practice, and I said, "Chris, were you a little nervous before taking that penalty shot?" And he looked at me, dead serious, and said, "Oh, I never get nervous." And I don't think he ever did get nervous. And I think some guys like to get nervous. So I'm not sure if anything like that is anything but an individual situation.

JL: Your national championship in 2009 was a remarkable study in determined focus—you're down two goals to Miami late in the third period, you rally to tie the game late, then you win it in overtime. Can you describe the emotion and the type of focus your team had as you saw it unfolding on the bench?

JP: Well, first of all, don't underestimate the idea of good fortune. We were hemming and hawing about whether to pull the goalie at that time, there were three minutes to go in the game. We're down by two goals, you've got to get two and you don't want to go down by three goals. There was a TV timeout, and I couldn't make up my mind. And so I decided, we're not going to pull the goalie, go ahead back out. And they went out, and then as they were going back out, they're about to drop the puck, and I realized, my assistant coaches are still pushing me to call a timeout. And so I kind of wasted a timeout because I could have made that decision during the TV timeout. So I called the timeout, and fortunately, we had worked on our 6-on-5 quite a bit at the end of that year. The guys knew what they were doing, and we were fortunate that we had the right guys out there—we had a lot of talented guys out there at the time. And they made some big plays—big plays at the right time. And the puck bounced for us a couple of times where they had chances to get the puck at an open net and they didn't. And then we made a couple of great plays—two unbelievable plays—to tie it up. Both within the last minute, we got two goals to tie it up. And then in the overtime, it was just a shot from the point that hit off a guy, the goalie never saw it and drifted over to him, so that was a good fortune kind of thing. It's happened to us in the past where we've won some big games late by overcoming some difficulties, and I do think that most of the time it's because big players step up in big times, and sometimes the other team gets jittery. Sometimes the other team thinks, "We're all set now." The worst thing you can ever say to yourself is, "We're all set now." And I think that might happen once in a while too.

JL: If your team's focus veers offtrack during a game or during a season, what types of strategies do you use to get things back on track?

JP: Well, during the course of a game you've got to get a feel for, say, things aren't going well, you may have to call your only timeout. You might wait until the end of the period and into the dressing room and read them the riot act. That works well once in a while, but most of the time it's more of a, "Come on, guys, we're better than that, here's what we're doing wrong" type of thing.

We only made one mistake that period, but we made it over and over and over again. If we can fix this, we're going to be real good. But also, I think you have to leave it up to the leaders in the dressing room. The chemistry in the locker room is important, the leadership in the dressing room is important, once you have your day, you've got to make sure that they are saying something too and that they are stepping up and pushing their own teammates. Motivation comes from within. I don't really believe in pep talks to tell you the truth. I've probably tried to give a few in my day, but I don't think they really work. I think motivation is from within, and I think certainly more so from peers than from coaches.

JL: Lastly, to wrap things up, in a nutshell, let's move away from hockey for a minute. How can the average person develop their ability to increase their focus and sharpen their powers of concentration in any area of life?

JP: I think you've got to get rid of clutter. You have to have planning. Preparation gets you focused. So if you've got a big meeting on Tuesday, then you can't be at the Red Sox game on Monday night. You might want to get ready for that. Sometimes you might tell yourself, "You're about to go into that meeting on Tuesday, and I wish I'd done a little more preparation last night for this."

Like we talked about in-the-week preparation for hockey, if you've done the right
stuff, if you've taken the right step, if you've
gone from checkpoint to checkpoint where
you're ready, the probabilities are you'll perform well.

Closing Thoughts on Focus

Focus is like a laser beam, a level of concentration that is required
to achieve optimal success. One of my favorite references relative to
the topic of focus is the concept of living in the present moment.
Dale Carnegie talks about living in "day-tight compartments"—shut
out the past and think not about the future. Or to be more precise,
have no anxiety about the future. The only way to achieve success is
to focus on today's work brilliantly—hour by hour, minute by minute. Don't let distractions get in the way, as they will try to do. Keep
those blinders on to ward off distractions.

I also believe in the power of questions to change what you
focus on. Studies have proven that the human mind can only focus
on one thing at a time. To quote another great personal development
author, Anthony Robbins, questions change what we focus on. Ask
yourself the right question in any situation, and you'll always get a
quality result.

Coach Parker talks about the relationship between preparation
and focus, too, and knowing what you are likely to experience in a
given situation through the preparation process increases your ability
to concentrate on what really matters. We see examples all the time
of athletes who are able to block everything out when the pressure is
on—except the task that needs to be accomplished. Closers in baseball are a perfect example—the game is always on the line for them,
and they have the ability to block out sixty thousand screaming fans
and concentrate on facing the batter.

The most focused athlete I have ever experienced in college
hockey was Joe Cannata, arguably the best goaltender in the history
of the Merrimack College men's hockey program. Joe was never rat-

tled about anything. If he gave up a goal, he would instantly develop amnesia and immediately block out everything and become a rock again. Joe instinctively had the type of perception that he lived in second-by-second airtight compartments. And you could tell a lot about Joe—as you can tell about any other goaltender—by his body language. He was intensely focused every single second of every single game.

I'll close this chapter by relating a quote from the TV series *M*A*S*H*, a quote attributed to the character of Charles Emerson Winchester, a surgeon at the 4077th. When first meeting his fellow surgeons in the operating room for the first time, he told them, "I do one thing at a time, I do it very well, and then I move on." While I certainly do not advocate such a brash and obnoxious approach to life, you get the idea. Focus your mind on only your task of today, one at a time. Do your very best at it and ask yourself the right questions. That's what makes a total winner.

C H A P T E R   9

Discipline and Self-Control

Dick Umile, University of New Hampshire

Dick Umile is a six-time coach of the year in Hockey East and is entering his twenty-third season as UNH head coach in 2013–14. He picked up his five-hundredth career victory on October 12, 2012, in a UNH victory over St. Cloud State. He has guided UNH to four Frozen Four appearances, eighteen NCAA tournament appearances, and twenty-four Hockey East tournament games. He has coached ten Hobey Baker finalists and twenty-eight All-Americans. He coached UNH to the national championship game in 1999 against Maine, losing in overtime. He also won the Spencer Penrose Trophy as National Coach of the Year in 1999. Coach Umile retired after the 2017–18 season, finishing his career with 598 wins.

In this chapter, we will look at the topic of discipline and self-control. A common thought regarding discipline is it is the process of staying on an even keel and not letting your emotions get the best of you. For this chapter, I traveled up to Durham, New Hampshire, and sat down face to face with Dick Umile, the head coach of the UNH Wildcats. In the 2011–12 season, UNH was the least penalized team in the conference, so it seemed appropriate to choose this topic for Coach Umile. I'll wrap things up at the end of the chapter with closing thoughts.

> JL: Let's start with the will to have a disciplined approach in our endeavors—that's sometimes not an easy thing, whether it be in college hockey or in life. Let's begin with the mindset of how you feel it's best to achieve a disciplined type of approach. What type of a thought process does one need to achieve the goal of being disciplined on a consistent basis?

> DU: Well, I think we all have a goal we want to reach, and we know there are going to be challenges along the way and you need discipline—with that being said, they have to understand what is expected of them, in whatever disciplined role they are involved in—that being not taking penalties during a game, discipline in their training, and the discipline in their emotion during a game. But they have to understand what is expected, individually and as a team.

> JL: In the game of hockey, invariably there are situations that occur during the course of a game in which your commitment to discipline sometimes can be tested—among those bring scrums after the whistle, for example. How might a player instinctively train himself to walk away from those types of situations when it is really is a heat-of-the-moment type of decision?

> DU: Well, it's difficult, but I think part of the training is how it affects them—the energy,

the emotion that they are involved with that takes away the productivity of what they are trying to accomplish. And I think it's a constant reminder—stay out of it, move forward. It affects other people, the emotions that you're involved with at the end of a scrum—not only yourself but it's affecting other players, your linemates, the team, the bench. So it's really just a matter of you having to discipline them, and if they continue to do things like that, then they're going to miss out on opportunities to play.

JL: When things aren't going so well, frustrations can sometimes lead to behaviors on the ice that illustrate being out of control. What types of messages do you relay to your UNH teams to avoid those types of situations, and what's the message when it does happen?

DU: The message is, you sit them. They're going to miss shifts. You're sending a message to them as well as to the other players on the team. And you learn very quickly when you're sitting on the bench; that's the best message you can send.

JL: Your 2011–12 team here at UNH was a shining example of outstanding discipline and self-control. The Wildcats were the least penalized team in the league, and you also had the least amount of average penalty minutes per game. That really seems like something the Wildcats took to heart. How happy were you and your coaching staff

with those numbers and how much of a
source of pride was it?

DU: Well, you know, I think we know we can
play the game hard and physical, and yet
try to stay out of the penalty box and not
get needless penalties—you know, selfish
penalties. We've tried to really take that
out of our team. There's going to be penalties from physical play, that's going to
happen—but the frustrated kinds of penalties that we really try to eliminate. That's
through self-control and that's through the
discipline we just talked about, but we had
a pretty good team. And if the leaders on
your team are disciplined, obviously your
captains, then it trickles down. And so I
think that's the best way to approach it, and
everybody kind of falls in line with that.

JL: Getting back to self-control for a minute,
is it fair to say that the time to address the
importance of staying in self-control is
before a situation occurs and to be properly
prepared for it?

DU: Yes, I think you talk about it, and there
are goals that you set for your team, and
goals individually that players should set
for themselves and how they should play, so
that you don't get into those frustrating situations. And it's easier said than done, but
you've got to work at it. And again, with the
discipline, that's all a part of the preparation. And then you won't even get involved
in those situations.

JL: Certainly this concept extends beyond hockey to real situations too—and for our purposes, we're talking about life away from the rink, in terms of social and classroom type situations, anything that a college student might encounter. How do you address maintaining and keeping that discipline and focus on those other types of areas?

DU: It's always a challenge, but it all starts in the recruiting process. Once you get to know players and recruit certain players, then you want to recruit those kinds of players. You meet the family, you see how they are brought up, you talk to their coaches and the teams that they played for to see how they've done all that, and that's all part of the recruiting. But off the ice, socially and off-campus, that's a constant. We talk about that on a daily basis—in the locker room, pre-practice, what's expected of them in the community, how they handle themselves. And hopefully it's just constant education in what is expected of them.

JL: The offseason is a time where discipline is so crucial- the players away from the daily grind of the regular season. Certainly it is a different type of ritual for these guys. How do you and your coaching staff instill the process of staying disciplined during this time when you're not in constant contact with the team?

DU: Well, these individuals are very talented players—they all have a goal to play professionally. The training, it's twelve months. Even when they're not playing with us, they're working hard in the offseason in their preparation, and that's all part of the discipline as well. So it's a time for them to relax as well and enjoy the offseason. We're not so concerned about them skating—we're concerned about the constant discipline of training off-ice, socially as well as physically.

JL: Who was your role model in shaping your personal philosophy regarding self-control and discipline and why?

DU: It was my high school football coach, Joe Hogue. He was a real disciplinarian. I think most, maybe 90 percent of your athletes, want discipline. I think young kids want discipline, and he taught us discipline—us knowing our plays, us being on time, all the little things—and practices were tough. And you had to be disciplined to get through it and become a good team and a good player. And that was on a daily basis in practice, and we practiced it every day. And then the game was easy, and it was fun.

JL: Mario Lemieux always demonstrated a cool, calm demeanor on the outside, never getting rattled, always giving off an air of quiet confidence and poise. Do you feel that that's a valuable trait to adopt as a hockey player to aid in helping with discipline, and if so, do any of your UNH players demonstrate that as a strategy and can you give an example?

DU: There's no doubt about it, I think he's a great role model. And if you can do that, you can compete and be physical and play hard, yet control your emotions and your frustrations. We have Connor Hardowa who's our captain next year—he's as big and as strong as any player in the league, yet he has complete control of his emotions, and you won't see him taking selfish penalties. And again he's one of the leaders so he leads by example.

JL: To wrap things up, let's move away from hockey for a moment and discuss how anyone can master the concept of discipline and self-control in any area of their lives. One of the most common real-life situations associated with this concept of weight loss and having the discipline to stay away from bad foods, for example. What advice might you give people on how to develop and maintain discipline, will, and self-control?

DU: I've often said this—you know, the military, to me, I think every kid should take a year and go into the military because that's where they learn discipline if they don't have it, and it works. To do that discipline, whether it's weight loss, whether it's your emotions, or whether it's physical training, I don't think you can be successful without discipline.

Closing Thoughts on Discipline and Self-Control

To a large extent, discipline involves looking at the big picture. It involves not doing something that you know will cost you or your team in the grand scheme of things. The root of this can be traced back to the Bible—turn the other cheek and walk away. To me that's the essence of what discipline is—having the strength to walk away from things that will harm you and the strength and character to move toward something that will empower you over the long haul.

Coach Umile talked about the need to stay away from selfish penalties on the ice, and it is so true, winning hockey games is hard to do when you are shorthanded and in the penalty box all the time. It takes great character to walk away when an opposing player is punching you in the back of the head. But if you are in control, and you develop that control to walk away, you'll wind up with the power play and your chances of scoring and succeeding will multiply.

In my own experience, I, like many other people, have struggled with managing my weight in past years. I never had the discipline to choose foods and healthy habits to serve me. There was no discipline and no self-control. I would always choose bad habits over good ones, always choosing short-term pleasure with my diet over the long-term pain and suffering of being overweight. That changed for me the moment I got a call from my doctor one day; I'll never forget it. My blood sugar was sky high, and he started to talk to me about the D word, diabetes. That's all I needed to hear. From that moment on, I became determined to gain control and discipline over my diet. I stopped drinking soda cold turkey and have not had a drop of it since (I used to drink regular Coke every day and with high frequency). I joined a gym and dropped fifty pounds, and I exercise regularly now. The threat of a health problem changes your focus very quickly, and you then change your perspective rapidly.

I also once read a story about a recruit in the United States Marine Corps who was stationed at Parris Island, South Carolina. The story was related in a book called *Corps Values* by Zell Millar, a former Marine. They were on a training exercise, and it was in the heat of summer. The recruit was dressed in full combat gear. He was crouched low at this position when all of a sudden, a large swarm of sand gnats descended on him. He instinctively began to swat at the insects, trying to shoo them away. His drill instructor happened to be nearby, saw him do this, and angrily told him to stop swatting at them. His exact words were, "You've had your chow, now let them have theirs." Swatting at those flies was paramount to giving away his position to the enemy, and of course that could lead to injury, or worse, death. Imagine having developed your discipline and self-control to the point where you can ignore the pain and discomfort of scores of insects biting and attacking you, while still keeping your eyes on the prize—that is the essence of discipline.

Discipline and self-control are also synonyms for the word poise. It means keeping your wits about you when everything around you is crumbling. Al Michaels demonstrated a great example of this during the 1989 World Series, broadcasting for ABC when the Loma Prieta Earthquake struck and rocked San Francisco's Candlestick Park and the entire Bay Area. In spite of the carnage around him, Al knew he had a job to do. He reported from the scene to the national audience with devastation and destruction everywhere. He instantly went from being a sports broadcaster to a news reporter in an instant. In my own experience of broadcasting, I've done games where I've lost Internet, phone lines go bad, and all sorts of technical problems occur in the middle of a game, but the key is to keep your mind on your task and have the discipline and self-control to do your job and not let your emotions get in the way.

Discipline and self-control are essential character traits. In hockey, as in life, the winners possess an uncanny ability to master this all-important skill.

C H A P T E R   1 0

Confidence

Jerry York, Boston College

Jerry York enters his forty-first season coaching college hockey in 2013–2014. He became the most winningest head coach in NCAA hockey history in 2012–2013 with a 5–2 win over Alabama Huntsville on December 29, surpassing Ron Mason's mark of 924 wins. He is one of only three head coaches to lead two different teams to national titles, taking Bowling Green to the national title in 1984 and then leading Boston College to the national title in 2001, 2008, 2010, and 2012. Coach York earned the Spencer Penrose Trophy as National Coach of the Year in the 1976–1977 season. He has been Hockey East Coach of the Year twice and has led BC to eleven NCAA tournament berths and has been a head coach of college hockey teams since the age of twenty-six. (*Author's Update*: Jerry York retired after the 2021–2022 season, finishing his career with 1,123 wins as a college hockey coach, 656 of those wins coming at Boston College. As of this writing, he is the only head coach in the history of Division 1 college hockey with 1,000 wins or more. He also finished his coaching career with five national titles, four of those attained in BC).

For the tenth chapter, we'll talk about the subject of confidence. This is such an important topic in our lives, and what better person to deal with on this topic than Boston College head coach Jerry York, a man who won three national titles in five years. Boston College won nineteen consecutive games enroute to their fourth national title under Coach York in 2012, in the process displaying an unshakable level of confident play along the way. When Coach York has finished his thoughts, I'll summarize at the end of this chapter with closing thoughts.

> JL: Confidence is an important topic and it's certainly relevant to performance on the ice. Let's start by asking, do you feel that gaining confidence in your approach to playing winning hockey is cultivated more by focusing on preparation or execution, or do you feel it's a combination of both?

> JY: You know, it's an interesting topic, John, confidence, because in all levels of life, I think it's extremely difficult to be successful if you don't have confidence in yourself, or you don't have confidence in your teammates in terms of the leadership in your locker room. We really try to instill confidence in our players, in our program, in our team, but I think you have to look inward and have self-confidence. And as you go through life, you can see people that are maybe nervous because they don't feel quite as confident on a subject they're talking about, or "Can I play at this level?" So I think confidence helps you execute. So for example, the Ryder Cup yesterday, whether it's a four-foot putt or a six-foot putt, by Kaymer to win the Ryder Cup for Europe, if he doesn't have confidence to make that putt, most likely his prediction is going to be how he feels—I'm not very con-

fident in the six-footer, I'll probably miss it, and sure enough, that speaks volumes on what will happen. But yes, I think you have to have confidence in yourself, and I think that can also spread among your teammates also.

JL: What do you feel is the relationship between preparation and confidence? Is it fair to say that the more prepared you are, the more likely your team will play at its best when the puck is dropped?

JY: No question. To be confident, you've got to feel like you've been there, done that. You've got to have been successful in situations so you can recall back when, for example, this was a tie hockey game and we had to kill a penalty to keep it tied as we have confidence to think back. I think confidence is a terrific subject, John, and it's probably overlooked when you start thinking about execution of forechecks and power plays and how to win hockey games. Some people call it swagger. I think if you're prepared and if you've worked hard in practice, if you've done all the things necessary to bring it to this level. I think preparation certainly breeds confidence.

JL: How do you as a coaching staff reinforce confidence in your teams here at BC? Is it just a case of winning building that feeling of confidence? Or is it more involved?

JY: The chicken before the egg, everyone seems to talk about it. In terms of the confidence level, you almost have to feel that you're a good player—coaches have to show that they have confidence late in a game. For example, can I put a freshman out there on the ice late in a game? That builds confidence. "Coach used me late in the game to kill a penalty, and it wasn't a 6-1 game, but it was a very close game," for example. I think you can instill confidence that way, but you can also take it away from kids, too, so you have to be very careful. It's a dynamic that's hard to put into words, but you can kind of look down at the bench and who has that confidence? "Put me in there, Coach, my eyes are ready to go." So it's a subject that should be brought up a lot in coaches' meetings and talked about with players.

JL: Last season, BC won their last nineteen games enroute to a national championship, but that seems like the perfect scenario where overconfidence could creep in. But with your team, it did not appear to. How do you guard against overconfidence during a long winning streak like that?

JY: Well, I certainly think you always have to be humble. You also have to always understand that your play is certainly based on inner confidence. You're always playing against good teams and good coaches, and other players on good teams that certainly are capable of winning hockey games. So I think overconfidence is a stumbling block. If you can't get by thinking that you have respect and you're humble at what you do for particular areas, this leads to overconfidence. We always try to instill confidence in our players, but also a healthy dose of respect for who we are going to play. And we'll be good and put ourselves in a position to win if we meet certain criteria—one is, hey, let's respect this opponent we're going to play—we're going to play at the best of our ability, so that's another area. Overconfidence can shorten up that winning streak pretty quickly.

JL: Many coaches, in terms of overconfidence, maintain that "one game at a time" approach (i.e., you can't look ahead). How much of that do you agree with, as it appears that looking past an opponent can really burst a bubble, so to speak?

JY: We talk a lot, John, about microscopic vision, vision through a telescope. You certainly have to have a long-range view here—our season goals, things I'd like to accomplish in the current year—but you also need to have a microscope where you are looking at each minute, each period, and each shift, and really focus on this opponent. But I think that it's a combination of both of those—certainly a long-range vision on where you'd like to go, your dreams, your aspirations—but also of this particular practice, this particular day, let's get better.

JL: Coach, Parker Milner was outstanding down the stretch a season ago. He seemed to be unstoppable at the end of the season. How infectious was his confidence on the team in front of him during that long winning streak?

JY: It's a perfect example to bring up Parker because I thought there were stretches early in our season where he completely lost his confidence level, questioning himself like, "Can I play at this level?" What's happening here, I'm letting in some soft goals, and I think that type of situation was clearly a player that lacked confidence. We talked to Parker about that; in short, we think that he's a very fine goaltender. We recruited him very highly to come to BC. So it was, "Let's take a step back, Parker. We're going to play some other goaltenders for a while, and just watch, and really start working on your self-esteem." And gradually he got back to better practices. We put him in a game, he won a game against the University of New Hampshire, and each game kind of built on that. That's a clear example of a player who wasn't quite sure that he could play at this level. And he worked on his inner thoughts, and he developed the mental attitude of "Hey I've got to become confident at what I do, I'm a good goaltender." And we try to reinforce that. And it was a terrific example of a young guy that as the season went on became what he thought he could become.

JL: Does dealing with adversity teach a team about developing confidence? And if so, what do you think that is?

JY: I think you're going to have to deal with adversity, you're never going to go through a season where everything is sunshine. You're going to have some rainy days and stormy days, and I think it makes you better. It builds on your resolve. We talk a lot here about being steadfast—meaning, you're not going to budge, you're going to go straight ahead, good direction. You really need to be steadfast in your beliefs. I think the way that individuals and teams respond to adversity says an awful lot about the character and the confidence level of each player and each team you coach. So you don't welcome adversity, but you certainly don't shy away from it, because you know it's right around the corner.

JL: How do you go about repairing the confidence level of your team if it becomes shaky for whatever reason?

JY: I think you have to get back to your values. Confidence is built upon preparation. You know, let's get back to the good old-fashioned hard-work ethic, working on fundamentals to build the foundation of your team. You can get shaky and lose—certainly I've coached teams that have had multiple losing streaks—so you've got to sit down and say, "All right, we're going to stay steadfast here. We're going to be resolute and really get back to where we were." We're looking at winning championships and winning trophies, but we're not doing it this way, so then you gradually get better because you're gaining confidence because you've worked hard, and you've done things necessary to bring your confidence back.

JL: We talked a bit about preparation earlier. Now in the course of preparing for an upcoming game, how useful do you feel visualizing being confident in pressure situations is to winning hockey games?

JY: I think it's just like on the golf course—when you get on that first tee, if you're not confident you're not going to put it on the fairway, you're probably not going to. I think going into our particular games as you watch opponents, again, you respect your opponent, but you've got to be confident that this isn't a David and Goliath thing. You feel like you're good and you have good teammates with you, and we really work on that with our club, you know. Let's play well where we expect to win, and we expect to be good tonight, so let's be all those characteristics to go along with that, and one of them would be certainly we're going to be confident that we're going to play well.

JL: BC hockey has enjoyed a great amount of success over the years, and you've certainly had a huge hand in that. To what extent does referencing the past successes of teams at BC help to instill confidence in your teams? Is that a motivational strategy that you like to employ?

JY: You know, I think each year is a new year. But I also think that there's a lot of carryovers over the years. We talk about leadership here as being really important to our team, and we can reflect back on some terrific leaders of the past, and someone they can emulate. We can talk about players like Brian Gionta, Patrick Eaves, and players of that ilk that really played well in big games. So I think the history of your program certainly helps. I know each year is new and you never know what to expect, but I think you can lean back on some prior teams that I think help an awful lot in your quest to achieve the goals for your next year's team.

JL: Stepping away from the rink for a moment, let's talk about the trait of confidence and how anyone can cultivate the attitude of confidence in any situation in life. What suggestions might you give to anyone looking to be more self-confident in any area of their life, no matter what the endeavor in life is?

JY: I think I had great parents that instilled in me the idea of "Hey, you can do what you want to do." It's a great time in your life, whether you're going to seventh grade and looking at some math situations, but just be confident that you can do the right thing. Make good decisions. I think your parents instill a lot of confidence in you, but other times I've seen players come broken families and have had different upbringings that have learned to emulate other people. They've read books, and they know how important confidence is just to be successful in life, let alone sports teams. I think you can develop it and look around and find some mentors that have it, and I think that's very important to look for mentors.

Closing Thoughts on Confidence

Confidence, in essence, is an attitude which is best cultivated through preparation. And the preparation I refer to here is mastering skills both personally and mentally to the point that you have a belief that you can execute your game plan with precision—to the point where you can see the results in your mind's eye. If you know beyond a shadow of a doubt in your mind that you can achieve something, you will be confident when the time comes. You will have the confidence to succeed because you have already seen it in your mind's eye.

I always like to refer to my broadcasting career when I talk about confidence because it is such an important skill, and the success I have achieved stems in large part from the preparation I put in. As I discussed in the chapter on preparation with Coach Whitehead, I put in hours of prep work prior to a game so that when it comes time to go on the air on Friday night for a college hockey game, I am confident it will go well because I know every detail has been covered. I know that nothing that will happen in that game will surprise me. And that includes not just the statistical work I do, but it also includes the mechanical work with the equipment. At this level, we are not provided with engineers, so it is also my responsibility to know everything there is to know about the broadcast equipment and the inherent problems that might occur during a broadcast. If a glitch occurs during a game, I do not get rattled because I know how to fix problems at the site. I have prepared for every contingency and am confident I can handle it if problems do occur.

Reference experiences are also a way to bolster confidence. Reference experiences are experiences in your past that demonstrate that you have the skill to succeed at something. Thinking back to a time in your life to when you succeeded at something gives you the confidence to handle it again in the future. This is where great coaching can be invaluable. The great college hockey coaches, such as Jerry York mentioned above, know how to motivate players by focusing on the types of things that their players have done well in the past to ensure future success.

To close this chapter on a college hockey note, there are many players I have come across in my time at Merrimack who have demonstrated an air of quiet confidence in how they have handled their affairs—Stephane DaCosta and Joe Cannata come to mind. But I also like to think of Kyle Bigos as one of the prototypical examples of confident living and playing. Here is a player who is the total package on the ice, who demonstrates his commitment to confidence by his leadership and physical style. No opposing player will take liberties when Kyle is in the area without paying the price, and his teammates feed off of that and it increases their confidence level. It's a mental attitude to be sure, and one of the most important ones to cultivate. Muhammed Ali was the symbol of confidence when he was in his prime, and his boasts were not hollow or empty. Ali would proclaim that he was the greatest in the world, but he also had the ability to back it up.

CHAPTER 11

Mental Toughness

John Micheletto, University of Massachusetts

John Micheletto began his first season as head coach of the University of Massachusetts in 2012–2013, steering the Minutemen to a mark of 12-19-3 in his inaugural campaign. Coach Micheletto spent nine seasons at the University of Vermont prior to coming to Massachusetts and has twenty-two years of coaching experience on the bench. He is the thirteenth head coach in program history. He also coached at Notre Dame from 1999 to 2003 and at Union from 1996 to 1999.

Chapter 11 deals with the concept of mental toughness, a vital trait to athletes and a skill that is crucial to performing at your very best. In this chapter, we will explore how to remain focused and determined when distractions occur and how to keep that edge when you need it most. I was very pleased to discuss this topic with UMass head coach John Micheletto, who replaced Don (Toot) Cahoon as the bench boss following the 2012–2013 season. After we hear from Coach Micheletto, I'll come back and finish off the chapter with my closing thoughts on mental toughness.

> JL: Coach, let's talk about this concept of mental
> toughness. It's a concept that many people

are familiar with, yet it's not easily understood. What is your perception of mental
toughness and how would you define it?

JM: Well, I think the biggest thing, at least as it
applies to the age group that we work with
in our sport is one, the ability to block distractions out. You know, with guys at our
level, there's a lot of things we're asking
them to do, not only on the ice but in the
classroom and in the community around it.
So when they come to the rink, to be able to
have the mental discipline and toughness to
block things out that might be a distraction
or might be weighing on them heavily and
focus on the task at hand. And then well on
the back end of it it's being able to step away
from both successes and failures and move
on as quickly as possible, and again, be able
to reenergize yourself and refocus for the
next task at hand.

JL: Well, you talk about distractions, and certainly there are quite a few, and a lot of these
athletes get bombarded from many different
areas, but how much of cultivating mental
toughness as an attitude involves being able
to filter out those distractions and focusing
on the end result?

JM: I think it's a huge part of a guy's success at
this level. I think everyone has a certain
level of it coming in, because in order to get
to Division 1 hockey, it's an important component to have had to develop. But to really
separate yourself as an elite player at this

level, I think it's one of the most important things that guys really have to focus in on and be able to do in order to be successful.

JL: In the course of a college hockey season, John, setbacks do occur. What mindset does it take to bounce back from a setback and remain focused on the goals you want to achieve?

JM: Well, again, I think we talk about having a short memory, and that's the biggest thing that guys need to do, again, for good or for bad. We talk about it often, and whether it's as big as the day after a game and coming to the rink ready to practice and get prepared for our next opponent, or maybe it's from shift to shift being able to quickly forget about something bad that has happened or something that you failed to do, or the fact that you just scored a goal or made an unbelievable play to set up a teammate, your memory has got to be very short because you've got to be able to move on and do it repetitively over the course of sixty minutes or over the course of thirty-four games of the season.

JL: Pressure is inevitable in any athletic competition. They say it can make you or break you. What strategies would you advocate to embrace pressure and make it work for you in the key moment of a game when the need to be mentally tough is at its highest?

JM: Well, pressure is a tough one. You talk a lot to your guys a lot about the old phrase of you want to apply pressure, not feel pressure. It certainly applies in all situations, but it's easier said than done, especially when you're an eighteen-to-twenty-four-year-old kid with a lot going on. So you use different strategies with different guys; obviously everyone responds differently in pressure situations; some guys you need to stay on because they need to stay riding that edge, other guys you need to be lighter with them because they're so wound up that you need to reign them in a little bit and bring them down a little bit. So I think from a pressure standpoint and how we handle our guys, it's an individual thing as opposed to a singular approach.

JL: What is the relationship between motivation and mental toughness in your view? How interrelated are they?

JM: I think that's an interesting question. Motivation is obviously high for our guys. It's probably the thing that they have the most of—their drive to succeed. So it's just a matter of whether that motivation compels your guys to embrace mental toughness training and embrace all it takes to become a mentally tough player. I think there is a correlation between the two, but I think, again, the difference is that your elite players are finding that link to drive them to be better and mentally tougher, and your average players that fall by the wayside at this level are guys that haven't been able to make that connection.

JL: One of the most common illustrations of mental toughness in hockey centers around goaltenders—when a goalie gives up a goal, he's got to forget it quickly and immediately refocus, like a closer in baseball forgetting a blown save. What is the key to a goaltender's ability to stay mentally tough when things don't go their way?

JM: (Laughs) If I had that answer, I'd be a millionaire right now, selling it to a lot of guys. As you mentioned, being a closer in baseball, or being a quarterback in football, or a goaltender in hockey, those are unique positions because of the spotlight really being on you. A lot of things could have gone wrong in front of you as a goaltender, but ultimately all the eyes are on you when the red light goes on behind you in a bad situation, or when you make an unbelievable save to bail your team out. So their mental makeup almost has to be different from everybody else's—sometimes you can hide as a player, and you can lean on your teammates a little bit more. So the goaltenders themselves, that's probably one of the reasons they are generally considered to be as quirky as it is, because it is such a tough and magnified position. But again, them more than anybody need to have that short mentality, and I think that's why you see, after most goals, you see most goaltenders have a little routine—and that routine for most guys after a goal is to get them mentally forgetting what just happened and moving on to the next step. And I think if you talk to any peak performance coach or any sports psychologist, that's something that they teach all their guys—that there's some tangible, tactical, or tactile way that they're moving on from one thing to another. And I think you see that exemplified more with goaltenders than anybody else.

JL: Let's talk about this UMass team—can you give an example of a player on your team who consistently exemplifies the practice of mental toughness and what makes him so good at it?

JM: Well, I don't know if there's one singular thing that makes this player that way. You know, Kevin Czepiel, our senior captain, is a great leader and a guy who I think has a great approach to the game, both his mental approach and how he prepares himself physically. I think for Kevin particularly, he came to us as an older player; he was a guy who was forced to change his roles throughout the course of his high school and junior career, so he learned how to be a goal scorer as well as a role player. I think he knew coming into college that he was going to have to hone his craft in order to be an effective player at the Division 1 level, and so he really did embrace the connection between motivation and mental toughness, and I think he really embraced that as part of what his makeup is and his preparation. And that is why he is one of our co-captains, and again, a very effective and a very difficult player to play against at this level.

JL: A big part of mental toughness is the internal self-talk that goes on. What type of internal self-talk is necessary to becoming consistently good at mental toughness, and how do you eliminate negative thinking in the course of focusing on the task at hand?

JM: Well, that goes hand in hand with the short memory that we have talked about before, John, and one of the easiest ways to do that is, as you say, the positive self-talk—reminding yourself that you are a good player. Although you didn't have a good shift or make a good play or even have a good game, you know how to be an effective player and a positive contributor to the team. Unfortunately, in our world, there are a lot of people who are willing to jump up and give you all the negatives in what you do, so your biggest ally has got to be that voice inside your head. And that's an important and integral part of guys being able to be effective.

JL: Frustration can be a major challenge to remaining mentally tough. How do you as a coaching staff refocus the lens when your team is playing well, for example, and you're not getting the results you're seeking to achieve, and you see that frustration creeping in? How might that frustration affect the ability to stay mentally tough, and how do you address it?

JM: At least with the example you just talked about, it's human nature to want to be rewarded for deeds well done, and when that doesn't happen, it's difficult to handle. So we constantly harp on our guys about focusing on the process and not the product. Knowing that what you're doing is right, and it's the way to lead to success, and not to read the scoreboard and let the scoreboard affect our emotions. Again, it's easier said than done, but I think that really focuses guys on being in the moment and making sure they're taking care of the right process. Frustration, as you said, is inevitable. It's going to creep in when you don't feel like you're getting that reward. And the only way to make sure it's not creeping in is, again, focus on what's really important and the now.

JL: Finally, let's step away from the rink for a moment. What advice would you suggest for anyone in any walk of life to develop the trait of mental toughness?

JM: Well I think that some of the topics you touched on here are all components of it, and I don't think that it's any different in life or in business than it is in sports. Again, one, making sure that you've got goals; two, that you've got action steps to try to get yourself toward those goals that feeds into your motivation and your focus. And ultimately, it's about making sure that when you fall down, you've got a process that you're going to pick yourself up and refocus yourself. It is the positive self-talk, having an actual process that you can refocus what your goals are if the goal you had originally set was unattainable and that you're making sure that you are constantly giving yourself the best opportunity to advance.

Closing Thoughts on Mental Toughness

We talked about discipline and self-control with UNH coach Dick Umile earlier in the book, and this concept of mental toughness is very much tied in with those concepts. One of the most intimidating places to play a college hockey game if you are a visiting team is Conte Forum in Chestnut Hill, home of the Boston College Eagles. The fans are as into the game there as anywhere. Their fans are ready to pounce on any and every mistake the visiting team makes, especially the goaltender. As relentless as those fans are, players know they have to keep it within the glass. Every time a visiting goaltender allows a goal at Conte Forum, the fans derisively chant en masse, spewing verbal venom at him. Players and goaltenders have to block all that stimulus out—if you were to let that get to you, obviously, it would affect your performance negatively. And you see that phenomenon in virtually every arena you go to. Maine and Alfond Arena are another classic example.

I once saw an infomercial on television back in the '80s called *Amazing Discoveries* hosted by a man called Mike Levy. In this one particular episode, they had Harry Lorayne as a guest. Harry Lorayne is a world-renowned memory expert who teaches people how to be more productive using their memory, and as an aside, he teaches some pretty fabulous mental memory tricks. One of these tricks is the ability to completely memorize a deck of cards. They brought one of Harry's students in to perform the stunt, and as he was quickly going through the deck performing the memorization of the cards, Mike Levy was constantly jabbering in his ear trying to distract him from memorizing and focusing on the task. Undaunted, he was able to complete the task by blocking out the external stimuli and staying focused. He memorized every card perfectly.

Another shining example of mental toughness occurs when there is a medical emergency, a potential life-threatening situation. It is imperative that you behave with a collected head despite the chaos around you. Panic will only worsen the situation. Someone needs to take control and make the right decisions and take the right actions. This is where mental toughness comes in—being able to block out the chaos and take immediate intelligent action. Mental toughness, in its simplest form, is the ability to filter out external stimuli that can deter you from your objective, and the ability to focus on the goal and the end result of your process.

C H A P T E R   1 2

Communication

Mike Cavanaugh, University of Connecticut

Mike Cavanaugh enters his eleventh season as head coach of men's hockey at the University of Connecticut in 2023–2024. Hired in 2013 as the fourth coach in school history, Coach Cavanaugh guided the Huskies through a transition from Atlantic Hockey to Hockey East. He guided UConn to the Hockey East championship game in 2021–2022, losing to Massachusetts in overtime at the TD Garden. The team's twenty wins was the highest win total under Coach Cavanaugh since his arrival in Storrs. He won the Calhoun Community Service Award at the 2017 Franciscan Sports Banquet, the 2013 Terry Flanagan Award by the American Hockey Coaches Association, and then served as an assistant on Jerry York's staff for eighteen seasons at Boston College.

Communication is an important topic in our day-to-day lives. How we communicate our messages to the world is crucial. Taking the time and effort to communicate effectively could mean the difference between getting a promotion or getting fired, from getting a date to being passed over, gaining benefits in negotiations, etc. The verbal and nonverbal messages we send out to the world affect our quality of lives and the results we ultimately achieve in life. For this next chapter, I connected with the longtime head coach at the

University of Connecticut, Mike Cavanaugh, for his thoughts on this topic from both a hockey perspective and a real-life perspective. Listen in to Coach Cavanaugh's thoughts, and I'll be back to wrap up the chapter with my thoughts at the end.

> JL: When in the course of communicating messages to your UConn hockey team, what is important in terms of ensuring that your message is received, and how do you know they've gotten it?

> MC: Well, you don't always know that they get it. You know, I think in any aspect of life, communication is important. Whether it be with your children, with your wife, with your family, the athletic administration here, my assistant coaches, communication is vital to having any type of success in life. Otherwise, it will just be chaos. And you know, with my team, I always wanted to tell them that there is an open-door policy here. What I don't want is them to perceive something, and then start talking about it within the locker room with other guys, without coming through my door first. And making sure that their perception is actually reality. Because a lot of times, it's not. And I think that's really important. You know, they're certainly at a different stage of life than I am, and I think that's a key to coaching is always to be able to try and bring yourself back to an eighteen or nineteen-year-old and be in their shoes and understand why they might be perceiving something one way. And you know, that's what your assistant coaches are good for too—because they can pick up on

that stuff, and they'll let you know. But I just try to be as open and honest with all my players. I have found that when you don't sugarcoat anything—and sometimes it hurts—they don't like to hear it, and at the time, they might be upset with you, and that might last a while. But usually, as time goes on, and you have time to reflect, you can say, "Well, I might not have agreed with Coach, but I appreciated him not beating around the bush, or giving me some BS answer to a question I've had. I just find that always seems to be the best method of communication is just being direct.

JL: Mike, do you have to take into account different learning styles when you're communicating to your players? For example, some are visual learners, some are auditory, etc. Do personalities factor into it at all?

MC: One hundred percent. You know, I had a player who was constantly screwing up drills. And what I didn't realize was, he wasn't an auditory learner. He couldn't just hear what I was saying and comprehend it. He had to see it. So with him knowing that, anytime there was a drill that we hadn't done in a while, or that was new, I made sure that I wasn't just saying like, "All right, defensemen down here in this corner, forwards up here, you're going to pass it." I'd write it out on the board so he could see it. And I think that was helpful that way. You also, I think when communicating, you have to understand different people's personalities. There are some people that you can be very direct with, and sometimes, harsh isn't the right word, but authoritative with your tone, and there are others that you can't. That's not going to work. That method of communication, they're going to take personally, and it won't be effective. They're not going to hear anything after you start talking because they're already feeling inadequate or hurt in that situation.

JL: Mike, how would you describe your communication style as the head coach of UConn hockey?

MC: I think the best communicators are great listeners. So I try to make sure that my players always understand that they have a voice. I might not always agree with it, but they have the ability to have a voice, and that's not always easy. I just think that that the days of Bobby Knight, where it's my way or the highway, I just think that's a really tough way to coach today. I just don't think that's as effective. I think you need to have communication as a two-way street. And it can't be a four-lane highway going out and a one way coming in—it has to be equal access for both parties for it to be successful.

JL: Let's talk about communication on the ice itself. Could you describe examples of how communication takes place in game situations and how important are these interactions?

MC: You know, I'm more of a believer that the communication has to be done during the week. In the game, I always didn't want a coach on me and in my ear all the time. I wanted to play the game. And I think if you want to get maximum effort, and maximize the talent level you have, you have to trust your players and let them play the game. Now, in between periods I might say something, or if I see something, and again, it's got to be the right kid, and I might say something to him. It's just like a goaltender. You would never, if a goalie lets in a goal that they want back, you would never say to that goaltender, "That was a lousy goal, why did you let that in?" or "You've got to be better and stop that puck." He's going to be junk for the rest of the game. You've got to let him work his way through it. He knows. Listen, the really good players that you coach, they know when they've made a mistake. They don't need to hear it again. I do think that there's two things that I do not tolerate, and that's lack of effort and mental mistakes. For example, lining up in the wrong place, or if we're doing a 1-2-2 and you're doing a 2-1-2, those are mental mistakes and those have to be addressed. If you're not backchecking that has to be addressed. But if a guy misses a one-timer or makes a bad play, or he's trying to go top shelf and he rips it over the net, in between periods, I can say, "Fellas, we've got to hit the net." You know, we've got to do a better job hitting the net. But in that moment,

I don't think it's very effective during the game to be a color commentator.

JL: Yes. In terms of players, when they're on the ice in game situations communicating among themselves, like defensemen talking to each other—how does that play itself out?

MC: Yes, that's different. From player to player, there has to be communication. You're not going to be successful if you don't communicate. You can be the best players in the world, but you know, especially defensemen, because you have one defenseman who's going to be the eyes of the other defensemen a lot of times. Goalies have to be communicators. On the bench, if you see a guy's going to get hit, the bench needs to say, "Get your head up, be ready, keep coming." During the game, it's vital and essential that your players communicate.

JL: How important is it to encourage open communication, Coach, when your players need to communicate issues to you, and what strategies do you use to encourage the players to feel comfortable when they need to do so?

MC: Yes, I tell them all the time, my door is always open. You know, John, sometimes I try to say, "Listen, if you're going to go back to your dorm and bitch and moan about what happened today, and you're a teammate, and you're going to sit there and listen to another teammate bitch and moan, you're as bad as he is." What I'm telling them is, "You come to me. Don't go back to the dorm or to your parents and bitch and moan about the coach. Come right through my front door." Those are the guys I'm looking for. And when you encourage that now, if you're going to have that open-door policy, I think it's really important that you do sit and listen. And you don't say anything. You just let them talk. And maybe ask a couple of questions to get them to open up even more, but they have to feel like they're being heard. And then once that happens, John, you'll be surprised. Players will go back, and they'll be like, "Yeah, I talked to Coach, and he was pretty good about it. He didn't throw me out of his office. He didn't say I was crazy." Now, a day or two later I might readdress the situation with the player and say, "I thought about what you had to say, and I agree with you in this space, but right here, you know I can't acquiesce to these demands. That's not how things are going to work. But I did hear you, and I'll do a better job of communicating this aspect to you in the future."

JL: Mike, what role do your captains and leadership group play in developing and maintaining good communication skills?

MC: It's so important. Because if the players know that the captains are a conduit to the coach, they'll confide in them and trust them. A lot of times I had to make it that it was a captain's idea that we're not going to have practice tomorrow. He came in and he said, "We are a little beaten up." And since I trust that captain, John, I said to them, "You guys have the day off tomorrow." I read a great book once, I think it was by Mike Keenan. He would make it seem like it was a captain's idea when it was something he wanted to do anyway. And there's a psychological aspect to it too. It's funny, when I look back, there were times where I was in college, and I was 100 percent right in this area, and I know I was, and now I'm looking back on it twenty years ago, and I'm like, "I was an idiot in that situation." You can't see the forest for the trees. And it's not their fault, it's just experience. It's maturity. Just having lived through it.

JL: Mike, I know we touched on this a little bit, but sometimes communication can be difficult. Sometimes you need to have difficult conversations. What is your approach to having these difficult conversations with your players? A situation that arises that is difficult or sensitive, and you need to communicate that message, what would be the first and most important strategy to use?

MC: I think they're all different. Like you just said, some of them are sensitive. There's a difference between a sensitive conversation, because in that one you need to have empathy and kid gloves, and you need to be there for the player when it's a sensitive topic. That could be a kid going through his parents getting divorced, or dealing with alcoholism, or something that's very personal and sensitive. That's different from when you need to make a hard decision and cut somebody. Those are two different conversations. And you've got to be adept at both. And you know the one where you have to cut a kid, I think you've got to go in and rip the band-aid off and tell them exactly why you're doing it. I was in a situation once when I was an assistant coach way back, and the head coach was cutting a kid, and I learned from it. He didn't really give him the real reason why he was getting rid of him. He just wanted to get rid of him, and he just said, "Well, you're not good enough." And that wasn't the real reason. The real reason was, he didn't like his off-ice antics and he didn't think that was real healthy for the team. And I learned a lot from it, because it didn't work out, and there was backlash, because a lot of people aren't stupid, they understand what the real reason was. And there was a lot of damage control. And I learned a lesson. And the hardest thing I've always said is when people ask me, what's the difference between being an assistant coach and a head coach. How can you prepare an assistant coach to be a head coach? I said, "Easy. The next time you have to cut someone, have your assistant coach cut him." As an assistant, you don't really have to do that. You're their buddy. But as a head coach, that's probably the hardest thing I've had to do as a head coach. And I've found that when you do have to do it, and when the time comes for that, it's just about being very open and honest and saying this is why.

JL: And at the end of the day, the player will respect you more for having the ability just to be honest.

MC: They're not going to like you either way. It's breaking up with a girlfriend. They're not going to like you for the next five or six months. But as you said, as time goes on, and as they reflect on it, they'll appreciate the fact that "Coach didn't string me along and he didn't give me the old 'It's not you, it's me' routine." You have to be direct and honest.

JL: Coach, is there a player from your experience here at UConn that seems to embody the essence of good communication both on and off the ice?

MC: I've got one right now. Our captain, Hudson Schandor, is as good as anyone I've seen at it. I'm really fortunate. We have two captains this year in Hudson Schandor and Jake Flynn, and they're both different. Flynnie is a more direct communicator, and Hudson's very, very good at seeing both sides. And not really picking a side, but seeing both sides of an issue, because let's face it, not every side is black and white. There's a lot of gray in some things, and Hudson can see that and work through it. And let's find a common ground here. So I really appreciate both kids I have right now, and I've been fortunate and blessed. Wyatt Newpower was a kid here who, when it was time to be the heavy, he could be the heavy. When it was time to put an arm around a guy, he could do that. Which isn't always easy. So I've really been fortunate here to have so many great captains.

JL: Mike, when a strategic aspect of the game is introduced to your players, if players have input or want to suggest an idea or a possible modification to the plan, do you and your coaching staff encourage that, the idea being the open exchange of ideas?

MC: Absolutely. The old adage, John, is if I have an apple and you have an apple, and I give you an apple, and you give me an apple, we each have one apple. And if I give you an idea and you give me an idea, and I'm open to it, now we have two ideas. And I think two ideas are better than one. Now, it can become counterproductive—you can't have fifteen ideas. You'd need to pare it down. But I do think that the one thing I do appreciate about the players is I can implement any system I want. But they're the ones playing. And they're the ones involved in it and having to live through it and experience it and deal with the consequences, good or bad. So any good coach is going to listen to his players. And then you go back and watch the film. And you can say, "Oh, you know, they're right, this is happening here."

JL: Right, and that's your tangible proof, you're looking at the video.

MC: Yes. And it's interesting, you know, with Hudson I remember we were doing this defensive zone coverage and he said, "You know, there are some nuances that take a while to get used to." And I was like, "Really!" And he said, "Yes, the way you take pucks in this position." And I didn't think of it that way, I just thought about it as "You're in this position and this is how you do it." He was right, it is different. And for a new kid to come in, they have to learn that skill set. So I have a little more patience with new kids learning the system after that conversation.

JL: And they may be bringing a new viewpoint to you that maybe you hadn't considered, which goes right back to that exchange of ideas, and it might wind up making you better.

MC: Yes! No question. It's so different when you're watching from the top row as opposed to actually being there. You know, the experience for the Indy race car driver is way different than ours watching it on TV. They're in the vehicle. So yes, I think you have to listen to your players.

JL: Coach, to finish up, if we can move away from the rink for a minute, what suggestions would you give to people in any walk of life to try and become excellent communicators?

MC: Listening. I really believe listening is important, and I'm trying to get better at it, to improve upon it. Not being afraid to have the hard conversations. I have to have one now, and I've been putting it off—I have to call someone and tell them I can't play golf with them next week after I already said I could. I don't want to have the conversation, but I have to do it. The longer you put it off, the harder that conversation gets. I think being a good communicator is having the hard conversations and not procrastinating. If you want to be a good communicator, you can't worry about how the other person is going to feel. You can't control how they are going to feel. And in a lot of ways, how they react, they're not responsible for how I feel or how I would react. It is what it is, but a lot of times I think we put a large burden on how that other person is going to feel after the conversation on ourselves, and that's not fair. I just think that's probably human nature, and it's something that you have to avoid.

Closing Thoughts on Communication

Excellent communication involves being an active listener, as Coach Cavanaugh stated. It involves being receptive to the open exchange of ideas. In my experience, I have always found it beneficial to understand the learning style of the person receiving the message, which Coach Cavanaugh always alluded to. There are three primary modes of learning—visual, auditory, and kinesthetic, which refers to touch stimulation—pats on the back, a hug, things of that nature. Hockey is a very visual medium in terms of learning; during practices, for example, coaches will diagram plays on a whiteboard for all to see. As we discussed in the chapter with Coach Cahoon earlier, video sessions are also a common practice in not only college hockey, but all sports. Some players are auditory learners and can get it after hearing something just once. Some are kinesthetic learners—that pat on the back reinforces the message.

I'm a big fan of Dale Carnegie's book, *How to Win Friends and Influence People*. He describes a communication style in the book that is commonly referred to today as the "Sandwich Technique." Basically, the gist of the technique is this—you begin by expressing admiration and appreciation for the person and emphasizing their good qualities. The middle of the "sandwich" is where you bring up the area that needs to be addressed—you don't tear the person down but be direct and describe in detail how the person (or in hockey, the player) can achieve better results. You then finish by once again praising the person and encouraging them. Behavioral science has shown time and time again that a person responds far better to encouragement than to criticism.

Active listening involves reflecting back what the other person has said after the receiving of the message communicated. It involves the active encouraging of questions in a supportive environment. In hockey, as in life, if you're not on the same page, things can unravel pretty quickly. And that's the essence of communication—understanding. And it goes back to what was discussed earlier—deliver the message in a way that is meaningful to the listener. Hockey players practice all week long to ensure that everyone is on the same page, and they are communicating constantly.

My favorite communication story involves an experience I had growing up. As a young student, I sometimes struggled with mathematics. My Dad wanted to teach me math concepts in a way I would understand. A method that was meaningful to me, knowing that I was a huge hockey fan, he took a sheet of paper, drew a line down the middle, and on one side of the paper he labelled it "Bruins." And on the other side, he labelled a column "Islanders." I was a Bruins fan. When he quizzed me, if I got an answer correct, he would place a mark in the Bruins column. If I missed one, he would put a check in the "Islanders" column. There it was—a concrete way for me to learn, in a way that was meaningful to me.

Of course, messages from communication need not always be verbal. Paying attention to nonverbal cues is important as well. Things like a nod, a wave, a thumbs up, need to be acknowledged for their importance too. You see a lot of that, of course, when communicating online. There are emojis for everything now—to express any kind of emotion and activity you can imagine. So while it is vital to master the communication strategies in a verbal way, you can also use a subtle approach to express acknowledgement and support of a fellow human being.

So, in a nutshell, you'll become an excellent communicator if you respect people's learning styles and teach in a way that is meaningful to the listener, through both verbal and nonverbal modes.

CHAPTER 13

Pulling It All Together

It was certainly difficult to select only twelve concepts to discuss in this book. There was a process of elimination which was undertaken to decide which concepts to include. Honorable mentions left out of the discussion included humility (which coaches Bazin and York alluded to), passion, and persistence, to name just a few. I happen to believe very deeply in the trait of humility. As someone who has been involved with sports broadcasting for the past twenty-eight years, I know firsthand that opportunities can be taken away at the drop of a hat. As a broadcaster, you have to come into any situation realizing that any job can be taken away from you. It's happened to me three times (four if you count the one year I did as the public address announcer for the Worcester Tornadoes) through no fault of my own. All these three teams ceased operations—in Lynn, Massachusetts, Kalamazoo, Michigan, and Lowell, Massachusetts—and it drove home the point that you're never bigger than the game. College hockey, like any other sport, offers many opportunities to be humble.

With Merrimack, I have visited the US Military Academy in West Point, New York, three times. While the games there were of significance, of course, the more important aspect of the West Point experience was understanding the tremendous service and sacrifice of the United States Army, as illustrated only by a trip to West Point.

Coming to an understanding of what cadets experience in terms of their study schedules, hockey schedules, and their military responsibilities is an awe-inspiring experience, and also just knowing that these players will be deployed after their time at West Point is very humbling indeed.

Since the initial volume was written, several coaching changes have been made around the league. Jerry York, as stated earlier, retired as the winningest coach in college hockey history when he stepped down from Boston College. Jack Parker ended his illustrious career at Boston University and was succeeded by three former BU alums: David Quinn, who went on to coach at the NHL level and is currently the bench boss at San Jose; Albie O'Connell, who played for Jack at BU; and then Jay Pandolfo, the current head coach who also played for Coach Parker. Northeastern's Jim Madigan took the athletic director's position at NU and was succeeded by Jerry Keefe, who for a long time was Jim's assistant with the Huskies. Red Gendron succeeded Tim Whitehead at Maine and sadly passed away suddenly, to be replaced by former UMass assistant Ben Barr. Dick Umile stepped down from his illustrious career at UNH and was succeeded by one of his former players, Mike Souza, who played under him and played in the 1999 NCAA championship against Maine. Kevin Sneddon, after a long and excellent career at Vermont, moved on and was replaced by Todd Woodcroft, whose brother Jay coaches in the NHL with Edmonton. UMass also underwent a change, hiring Greg Carvel, who spent many years at St. Lawrence. Carvel brought the Minutemen to the promised land by guiding them to an NCAA championship. Merrimack parted ways with Mark Dennehy, who ascended to the NHL and the New Jersey Devils organization and replaced him with long-time college hockey coach and Dartmouth alum Scott Borek. Coach Borek guided the Warriors to their second NCAA tournament appearance in 2022–23 (the first being under Coach Dennehy), losing to Quinnipiac in the NCAA regionals. UConn entered the league guided by the study hand of Mike Cavanaugh, who you read about in chapter 12. At the time of this republication, two coaches still remain from the initial work— Providence's Nate Leaman and UMass Lowell's Norm Bazin. Notre

Dame also spent a brief time in the league before departing for the Big 10 conference, and we as media streamlined into a new world, moving from radio to television as we transitioned to ESPN+ starting in 2022—23.

All the content in the original volume is here in the updated work. The UConn chapter was added for the newer version, as the Huskies were not a member of Hockey East when the book was first written.

It is my hope that in this book I have tried to cover some of the more important traits that we encounter in our everyday lives. The twelve men I interviewed for this book are all men of high character and have all recorded success in their own way. I hope that sports lovers and non-sports lovers will all benefit from the book, because I think there is something within these pages for everyone.

If this book has touched you in any way, please let me know. I answer all correspondence. Feel free to send me an email at jleahybroadcaster@gmail.com or visit me online at www.johnrleahy.com. I hope that whatever game of life you play, you'll be your own champion, just as the coaches of Hockey East are.

I'll see you out at the rink.

John Leahy
Merrimack College Hockey Broadcaster,
Men's and Women's Hockey, ESPN+

REFERENCES

During the course of this work, there were publications I used to illustrate examples regarding topics. I would like to recognize these publications here and give thanks to the authors for serving as a critical point of inspiration to me.

Carnegie, Dale. Originally published in 1936. New York: Simon and Schuster.

Robbins, Anthony. *Awaken the Giant Within*. Copyright 1991. New York: Fireside Publishing.

Miller, Zell. *Corps Values: Everything You Need to Know I Learned in the Marines*. Copyright June 25, 1997. Longstreet Press.

ABOUT THE AUTHOR

John Leahy is the play-by-play voice of Merrimack College Hockey. He provided play by play for the men's team on radio from 2005 to 2022 and transitioned to provide television play by coverage on ESPN+ in 2023. He also began with television play-by-play coverage for the women's team in 2023, also on ESPN+. He also has sixteen years of play-by-play experience in minor league baseball, working with teams in Massachusetts, Michigan, and Kentucky